VIDEO POKER
· AND ·
SLOTS
FOR THE
WINNER

ABOUT THE AUTHOR

Marten Jensen, the "Doctor of Gambling," is one of the foremost authorities of gambling in the world. An expert on all the casino games, Jensen is also the author of the following books on beating the casinos, all published by Cardoza Publishing.

Cardoza Publishing Books by Marten Jensen
Secrets of the New Casino Games
Secrets of Winning Roulette
Video Poker & Slots for the Winner
Beat the Slots
Beat Multiple Deck Blackjack
Beat the Craps Table
Casino Gambling Secrets

VIDEO POKER

· AND ·

SLOTS FOR THE WINNER

MARTEN JENSEN

CARDOZA PUBLISHING

SECOND EDITION
4th Printing

Copyright© 1999, 2002 by Marten Jensen
-All Rights Reserved-

Library of Congress Catalog Card No: 2002101332
ISBN:1-58042-062-1

Visit our website or write us for a full list of Cardoza books, software and advanced strategies.

CARDOZA PUBLISHING
P.O. Box 98115, Las Vegas, NV 89193
Phone (800)577-WINS
email: cardozabooks@aol.com
www.cardozabooks.com

TABLE OF CONTENTS

INTRODUCTION

This book is going to show you how to win money playing video poker and slot machines! You'll learn how to select the best machines to play from the many choices available to you as a player, how to extend your bank-

roll, and how to use all this information to win as often as possible.

Even better though, if you follow our advice, you will not only cut the house edge to the bare minimum, giving yourself the best chances of walking away a winner, but under certain conditions, you'll actually have the advantage over the casino and the expectation to win money!

This book has been expanded to include the newest and latest winning strategies for *today's* machines, and has a ton of information, all written with you in mind. The advice is easy-to-read, practical, and can be used under actual casino conditions playing real machines. The winning strategies are based on sound mathematical principles, so that if you follow our advice, you'll be playing with the odds, not against them.

If you want to be a winner, then this is the book for you. Read on because we have lots to talk about!

BEATING THE SLOTS

Not all that long ago, there was little point to reading a book on slot machines—if you could even find one. Most of the games were very similar: they had three reels, a coin slot, a coin tray at the bottom, and an actuating lever at the right side. You just dropped in a coin and pulled down the lever. The reels spun around, and if you were lucky, you won a few coins.

Most people think that, unlike video poker players, slot players don't have to make any decisions—they just drop in coins and hit the SPIN button. WRONG!!! Slot players have plenty of decisions to make, and if they make wrong decisions, or arbitrary ones, they will rarely come out ahead. So what are these important decisions?

The first, and most important one, is the selection of the right machine. But aren't they all basically the same? Absolutely not! There is such a variety of slot machines in the casinos, made by numerous competing manufacturers, that some of them are bound to be better than others. The trick is to know how to tell the good from the bad. We show you how to find the best machines to play!

Once a suitable game is selected, your second decision is to determine how many coins or credits to wager on each spin. Today, there is no such animal as a single-coin slot machine. All modern machines take multiple coins, and the misguided advice to always bet the maximum can cause serious damage to your wallet. You need to know which games are best played with a minimum wager and which always require the maximum. Do it wrong, and you will reduce your chances of winning. We show you which games to play with a minimum wager and which require the maximum bet.

All the ringing bells, flashing lights, and clattering coins tend to mesmerize the majority of slot players. They sit at a machine and spin the reels as fast as they can, hoping they will win one of those big jackpots that they perceive are being won all around them. They believe that if they keep feeding the machine and keep those reels spinning, sooner or later they will also be big winners. And then they wonder why they keep on losing.

Once you have read and absorbed this book, you will look at those players and chuckle. They think slot machines are mindless games requiring no particular strategy, other than pure luck, and that some people are just luckier than others. But you will know better. You will know that by learning about the games and by using a methodical approach, you are much more likely to come out ahead than those poor, unenlightened amateurs.

BEATING VIDEO POKER

Although they were introduced in the 1970s, video poker games didn't get popular until the 1980s. By the 1990s, many slot players realized that video poker had become the most liberal type of slot game on the casino floors. As a result, popularity surged until it became a major segment of the slot machine business.

With perfect playing strategy, most video poker machines in Nevada pay back 97-99% and some even pay back more than 101%. It is easy to find non-progressive video poker games that pay back more than 99% when the player uses expert playing strategy. Furthermore, when the jackpot on progressive games builds up sufficiently, the payback can exceed 100% by a nice margin. We show you how to find the machines with the best paybacks and how to play them like an expert!

With the help of this book, the actual payback of any video poker machine can be determined. There is no guesswork. Every video poker machine has its complete payout schedule posted on the video screen or on the glass display above the screen. Using this information, the overall payback of that machine can be computed. But you don't have to do the math; it has been done it for you. This book contains over 90 payout schedule charts for different types of video poker machines. Each chart gives the overall payback percentage for perfect play and tells which playing strategy table should be used to get the best payback.

In video poker, the player has a measure of control over the outcome of each hand. After the deal, the player can try to improve the initial five-card hand by selecting any or all cards to be replaced by new ones. The new cards are then dealt from the same randomly-shuffled deck as the original five.

Obviously, to play it well requires the correct playing strategy. We provide you with complete strategy tables for every major video poker configuration found in the casinos.

WHY YOU SHOULD READ THIS BOOK

Just by thumbing through this book you can see that it is brimming with useful information about video poker and slot machines. When you read the details more carefully, you will learn how to select the best machines to play, how to minimize the casino's mathematical advantage, and how to extend your bankroll. We provide you with the information you need to win as often as possible.

Modern slot machines are no longer the mindless one-armed bandits of yesteryear. Now they are all sophisticated computer-controlled devices, although the ones with actual mechanical spinning reels do try to hide the fact that they are totally managed by the latest modern technology. So how does this affect the average player? It means that if you are not completely familiar with the game you are playing, and if you are not playing the best way possible, you will likely lose your money at a faster rate than the designed-in payback would indicate.

WHAT MAKES THIS BOOK SPECIAL?

Most books on video poker strategy try to *teach* you how to play like an expert. In order to accomplish that, they expect you to memorize the strategies and practice at home before you even walk into a casino. Some even try to teach you the mathematics behind the strategy calculations. Many say that you should concentrate on no more than two or three types of games if you expect to be successful. That sounds like a lot of work—just when you are trying to enjoy yourself.

This book has a different approach. It is not a textbook; it is a reference book. You should at least read the early chapters to gain a basic familiarity of the game and all its variations. But then, all you have to do is take this book into a casino and plop yourself down in front of a video poker machine.

Now look at the posted payout schedule and find the matching one in the book. The chart in the book will tell you the theoretical payback for that machine and which strategy table to use. If you don't like the payback, repeat the procedure at another machine.

You don't have to memorize a thing. Of course, if you play a particular type of machine often enough, you will eventually get to know the strategy—and *that* is the easiest way to learn. Furthermore, *this book contains no math*. All the math has been done for you, so that all you see are the results.

Once you are ready to play the video poker machine that you have selected and identified in the Payout Schedules chapter, it is important to use the correct playing strategy for that particular type of machine. As will be explained later, there is more than one approach to devising a playing strategy. The approach used in this book is based on exact probability calculations which are modified to simplify the strategy without significantly reducing its accuracy.

This approach generally results in fewer playing errors because the simplified strategy is easier to comprehend and use. Furthermore, simplification has yielded only 33 different strategies for over 90 different varieties of machines.

Yes, there are other books that contain charts of various payout schedules, but in most of them, matching a chart to a machine isn't very quick and easy. Since this book contains the largest number of payout charts ever published, a simplified approach had to be devised.

This book contains the largest number of video poker payout charts ever published.

You begin by looking up the basic game in the Payout Schedules chapter. After a short while, you will get to recognize the game types such as *Original Jacks or Better, Bonus Quads, Deuces Wild*, etc. At the beginning of each section, you will see a list of descriptive names such as *Double Bonus Poker, All American Poker, Super Aces*, and *Aces and Faces*. These names will help verify that you are in the right section of the chapter and you can then select a matching payout schedule.

Within the longer sections, the charts are arranged in a logical order as defined on the introductory page for that section. You can typically do this entire procedure in a few seconds. Then all you have to do is turn to the designated strategy table in the Playing Strategy Tables chapter and begin to play.

If you are a casual or recreational gambler, this book will help extend your bankroll and your playing time at the machines and will even help you to go home a winner. If you are a serious gambler or a professional, it will give you the information you need to maximize your return and limit your losses. Remember, unless you know how to effectively count cards at blackjack, there is no other game in the casino that provides you with more than 100% return on your money. In that regard, video poker is truly unique.

HISTORY OF SLOTS & VIDEO POKER

The slot machine was invented over 100 years ago in San Francisco where the first primitive nickel machines appeared in gambling halls and saloons. They soon became very popular and, in 1907, an enterprising fellow

> **OVERVIEW**
>
> Slot and video poker machines have become increasingly popular gaming devices, today, more so than ever!
>
> Let's see where it all began...

in Chicago by the name of Herbert Mills started manufacturing slot machines on a large-scale basis. Before long, Mills' slot machines were being distributed throughout the country and were installed mostly in saloons and pool halls.

By the 1930's, most slot machines were controlled by the mob. When Mayor Fiorello LaGuardia ran the slots out of New York City, the mob took them to New Orleans by invitation of Governor Huey Long, who made millions in kickbacks. Machines controlled by the mob had such a poor payback (typically about 50%) that they came to be known as "one-armed bandits."

Meanwhile, after Nevada legalized gambling in 1931, the first legal casinos installed slot machines for the purpose of distracting and entertaining wives and girlfriends while the serious gamblers played at the gaming tables. As more casinos opened, some of them began to view slots as a profit center and improved the payouts to attract more business. The improved payouts enticed some of the serious gamblers to the slots and began a long-term escalation in the popularity of slot machines. To this day, however, women continue to be the mainstay of slot players.

It is interesting to note that over the years the original concept of the slot machine has not significantly changed. Many of today's slots still have three vertical reels with various symbols, and an operating arm at the right side. Modern variations include machines with more than three reels, the ability to accept multiple coins (and bills), and electronic machines with video screens — but the basic form remains the same.

In 1975, the development of the first video machines by the Fortune Coin Company precipitated major variations from the traditional mechanical slot machine. In 1978, Fortune Coin was bought out by the Sircoma Company, later renamed International Gaming Technology (IGT), and the product line was soon expanded to include four-reel video slot machines. Although slot machines with video screens were not that much different than their mechanical cousins, they ultimately led to the introduction of video blackjack machines, quickly followed by video poker machines.

Neither type of machine was very popular at first. The meager payoffs for winning blackjack hands could not compete with the large jackpots of the regular slots—and still can't. The payout schedules of the early video poker machines were also not impressive, but this changed completely in 1979 when IGT introduced their Fortune Model 701 Draw Poker machine. The Model 701 came in several versions, some of which had the first 9/6 full-pay jacks-or-better schedule with an astonishing 99.5% payback. Many of these venerable machines can still be found in some of the older casinos.

After that, every time the payout schedules were improved, the game increased in popularity and, by 1985, it is estimated that over 25% of all slot machine players were playing video poker. Video poker had become the fastest-growing gambling game in the world.

WHY VIDEO POKER?

Although it took a while for the gambling public to warm up to video poker, once machines with improved payoff schedules were introduced, it did not take long for their popularity to accelerate. Why has video poker become so popular? For the following very good reason:

Most video poker machines pay back 97-99%, and some pay back more than 101% with perfect playing strategy.

Although some casinos may assert that their slots pay up to 98.5% or even 99%, pay attention to the "up to" part of that statement. The advertised payout usually applies to very few machines, and there is no way of telling which ones they are. Without knowing it, you can easily be playing a traditional slot machine that pays back only 85%. Video poker machines, however, are an open book.

The maximum long-term payback of any video poker machine on the casino floor can be determined.

This is not true for traditional slots. With the help of this book, however, you can find out the payback of any video poker machine by simply viewing its posted payout schedule. This knowledge will allow you to select the best machines to play. When you start playing video poker, you will realize that it is a game of skill because the player has an opportunity to improve the dealt hand by drawing replacements for any or all of the cards.

After the initial five-card hand is randomly dealt by the machine, the player gets to discard any or all of the cards, which are replaced by new ones. Choosing which cards to hold and which to discard to maximize the payback requires correct playing strategy. The main purpose of this book is to teach the video poker player how to optimize those choices.

Although there are many variations of video poker, almost all of them are based on a one-time replacement of any undesired cards in a five-card hand dealt from a randomly-shuffled standard deck of cards. This is the same basis as a form of poker called *five-card draw* or, simply, *draw poker*.

To better understand how to win, we will first present a brief review of the game of draw poker.

DRAW POKER - THE GAME

When the outcome of a game is based solely or primarily on the result of a random process, such as keno or the state lottery, it is legally considered to be a gambling game. If the outcome primarily depends on the proficiency of the players, such as bridge or tennis, it is considered to be a game of skill and local laws against gambling usually do not apply.

Because it is played in most gambling casinos, is played for money, and is illegal in many places, poker resembles a gambling game. The fact is that good and bad luck or the fall of the cards has only a minor effect on the outcome of a poker game. In the long run, the most skilled player will almost always win. It is interesting to note that, in California, the game of draw poker is legal because it has been acknowledged by the legislature to be a game of skill.

Although there are many forms of poker, we will only consider draw poker because it is the specific game that video poker machines attempt to emulate. Draw poker is played with an ordinary deck of 52 cards, or a 53-card deck if the joker is included. The ace is normally considered to be the highest value card and the deuce is the lowest. Any card or cards may be designated as *wild*, the most common being the deuce.

The game begins with an initial ante, where everyone contributes a fixed amount into the pot. Each player is then dealt five cards face down, followed by a betting interval. (Betting methods and strategy will not be discussed because video poker does not provide any subsequent betting opportunities.) When the betting is concluded, each remaining player may discard any unwanted cards, which will be replaced by the dealer with new cards from the deck. A second betting interval then occurs.

After the second round of betting, comes the showdown, in which all the active hands are displayed and the best hand takes the pot. If all but one player drops out during a betting interval, the remaining player wins by default and does not have to show his or her cards.

Although the above is an over-simplified description of poker that does not include the intricacies and psychological aspects of the betting process, the basic rules of the game are simple and easy to learn. The only other thing you need to know are the various card combinations that produce winning hands.

The relative value of a poker hand depends on which of the following card combinations it contains, listed in order from the highest to the lowest:

Five-of-a-Kind:

Five cards of the same rank. This is the highest-value hand in a game with a joker or wild cards. It necessarily includes at least one wild card, since a standard deck has only four cards of a given rank, one of each suit. The following example shows a five-of-a-kind hand of four queens and a joker.

Royal Flush:

An ace-high straight flush, as below. This is the highest-value hand in a game that has no joker or wild cards.

Straight Flush:

Five consecutive cards, all of the same suit. When the ace is part of the sequence, it is always low; if it is high, the result is a royal flush.

Four-of-a-Kind:

Four cards of the same rank. The fifth card is unrelated to the others.

Full House:

Three cards of the same rank and two of another rank, that is, three-of-a-kind and a pair.

Flush:

Five cards of the same suit, not in sequence.

Straight:

Five consecutive cards of mixed suits. An ace may be either the lowest card as in A-2-3-4-5 or the highest card as in 10-J-Q-K-A but not the middle (K-A-2-3-4 is not a straight, simply an ace-high hand).

Three-of-a-Kind:

Three cards of the same rank. The remaining two cards are unrelated.

Two Pairs:

A pair of one rank and a pair of another rank. The fifth card is unrelated.

One Pair:

Two cards of the same rank. The three remaining cards are unrelated.

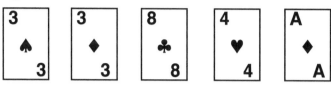

High Card:

The highest ranking card in a hand that does not contain at least one pair. The following hand, for example, is called *king high*.

The order in which the above card combinations are listed is not arbitrary, but represents the mathematical probability of being dealt a particular hand (before the draw). From a 52-card deck with no wild cards, for instance, you should expect to get dealt four-of-a-kind once in every 4,165 hands, three-of-a-kind once in every 47 hands, and a pair in every second or third hand. For those readers that are interested, the precise odds of being dealt various hands are shown in the Statistical Tables chapter.

Within one combination, the hand with the highest ranking cards is the winner. That is, a K-K-K beats a 9-9-9. Whenever two hands contain the same combination with cards of the same rank, the hand with the highest-ranking odd cards is the winner. For example, if two hands both have Q-Q, the winner would be determined by the highest rank of the remaining three cards in each hand. If two hands have identical 5-card combinations except for different suits, such as 2-3-6-8-Q of hearts (heart flush) and 2-3-6-8-Q of spades (spade flush), the pot is split. All suits in poker are of the same relative value.

The "jacks-or-better" rule is almost always followed in friendly home and family games. When this rule is in effect, a player cannot open the first round of betting without holding at least a pair of jacks. Thus, a pair of jacks is the weakest hand that can win the pot. Almost all the early video poker machines followed this rule so that the lowest paying hand was a pair of jacks. Jacks-or-better machines, as they are called, are still the most popular kind and will probably remain so in the future.

VIDEO POKER VS. DRAW POKER

Video poker is fundamentally a one-player video representation of draw poker. Aside from the fact that all the action occurs on a video screen, video poker has some significant differences from draw poker. To avoid falling into serious traps while playing video poker, it is important to be aware of these differences. This is especially true for players already familiar with draw poker, since they have likely developed particular playing styles and habits. Although the two games have many similarities, the playing strategies are quite different.

The most important point in video poker is that you are playing against a machine with a fixed payout schedule, and there are no other players at the table. In table poker, if your hand is better than that of any other player at the table, you win the entire pot. You could win with a very poor hand, if that is the best there is—or you could lose with a very good hand if someone else has a better one. To win a hand in video poker, it must simply match one of the hands defined on the posted payout schedule. You don't have to *beat* anyone.

Another important point is that the rank of a winning combination is usually immaterial. That is, three kings pay the same as three deuces, and an aces-up two pair pays the same as any other two pair. And finally, you can't fold your hand, so you must draw no matter how bad a hand you were dealt.

> *Mob-controlled slot machines paid out so seldom that they came to be known as one-armed bandits.*

Many of players who have never read a strategy book, such as this one, continue to apply their own draw poker strategy. They do things such as keeping an ace or face-card kicker when drawing to a pair. This fools nobody (there aren't any other players to fool) and, although it doesn't change the probability of drawing another pair, it greatly reduces the odds of drawing three-of-a-kind, four-of-a-kind, or a full house. In other words: *Never keep a kicker.*

In the table game, a player would normally drop out rather than draw four cards to a single face card. However, holding one face card is frequently done in a jacks-or-better game. And for a garbage hand that doesn't even have a low pair or a face card, it is appropriate to draw five new cards. These situations are all covered in the playing strategy tables.

VIDEO POKER & THE MACHINE

As with slot machines, to activate a video poker machine you must feed it money. Do this by sliding a greenback into a slot or dropping in one or more coins. A one-dollar bill will give you 4 credits on a quarter machine or 20 credits on a nickel machine, which you can then play in any desired amount, usually up to a maximum of five.

> **WINNING TIP!**
> If you're dealt a pat hand, be sure to press all five HOLD buttons and that the machine displays the word "HELD" before you press DRAW.

While inserting a bill will simply register an appropriate number of credits, dropping in one or more coins will actually start the machine. If you insert five coins or press the PLAY 5 CREDITS button, the machine will deal your initial hand automatically. Manual play buttons are typical on video poker machines, although most of the newer machines now also use touch screens.

If you insert fewer than five coins or enter fewer than five credits, you will have to press DEAL or

DEAL–DRAW to see your initial hand. The machine will then display five cards on the video screen, which constitute your initial hand.

Now, examine the hand carefully to decide which cards you want to save or discard. Do this by pressing the appropriate HOLD or HOLD–CANCEL buttons, which are approximately lined up with the cards on the video screen.

On machines with touch-sensitive screens, you can just touch the screen images of the cards that you want to keep.

You may hold or discard any number of cards you wish. If you change your mind, press any of the HOLD buttons (or touch the screen) again and the action will be reversed. On some older machines there is a separate CANCEL button that resets the HOLD buttons. Sometimes the HOLD buttons don't register correctly, so you should check to see that the word HELD appears by each card you intend to keep.

Note that, instead of HOLD buttons, some older machines may have DISCARD buttons, which act the reverse of HOLD buttons.

Should you be so fortunate to be dealt a pat hand, you must be careful not to inadvertently discard any of the cards. Although a few machines have a STAND or HOLD ALL button, on most you have to press all five HOLD buttons.

Be certain all five cards in your hand display the word "HELD" before you press DRAW. If you accidentally hold or discard the wrong card, don't feel stupid—we all do it sooner or later. It usually happens when you are tired or are playing too fast.

When you are ready to draw, press DRAW or DEAL–DRAW and every card that is not held will be replaced with a new card. This is your final hand. If it matches one of the payout combinations, the machine will automatically register the appropriate number of credits. On old machines, the winning coins will be dumped into the tray. The payout table is located on either a glass panel above the screen or on the video screen itself.

With some modifications, the payout schedule is based on the standard poker hands described previously. In games without wild cards, the minimum payout is usually for a pair of jacks although there are some machines that set the minimum at a pair of tens, a pair of kings, or two pair. For games with deuces wild, the minimum payout is three-of-a-kind.

Many games also pay bonuses for four-of-a-kinds of a specific rank or royal flushes with the cards in a specific order.

When you press the CASH OUT button, the credits on the machine will be converted to coins that will be dropped into the coin tray with a big clatter. You may press this button anytime between hands. Don't forget to press the CASH OUT button when you leave the machine, or someone else will do it for you.

VIDEO POKER - THE MACHINE

Externally, video poker machines appear to come in a great variety of types, styles, and flavors. Internally, however, they are all quite similar. Each one contains a specialized, dedicated microprocessor, along with its memory and support chips that control every aspect of the machine's operation. The major difference between machines is how the microprocessor is programmed.

Whenever a new hand is about to be dealt, the machine shuffles the deck electronically. To assure that the shuffle is done honestly, the poker program in each machine accesses a constantly-running random number generator to assure that the 52 cards (53 cards with a joker) in the deck are always dealt out in a random fashion. Fundamentally, the random number generator is a program algorithm within the machine's microprocessor that continually generates pseudo-random numbers.

To further assure complete randomness, the generator randomly accesses over a billion different number sequences and typically cycles through them at a rate of a thousand per second. Thus, there is no chance that the player can affect the randomness of the deal.

It is the programming of the random number generator that is of greatest concern to state gaming regulators whenever a new model machine is being evaluated. They examine the mathematical basis for the algorithm and verify, by testing, that the machine consistently deals random hands.

If the deal is random, and the machine payouts are in accordance with its posted schedule, then the player cannot be cheated. As a result, in states that have effective gaming controls (such as Nevada and New Jersey), the chance of encountering a rigged machine is almost non-existent. Unless you are playing in an illegal or uncontrolled gambling hall, don't worry about it.

Once the initial hand is dealt by the machine, there are two different methods employed for dealing out the replacement cards for the draw. In the method used by most early machines, ten cards are actually dealt out. The first five are the initial hand, while the second five are lined up and hidden behind the first five. The second five cards are the potential draw cards, one for each of the initial five cards of the hand.

Then, for every card that the player discards, the card that was hidden behind it is exposed. For each card that is held, the backup card remains hidden.

In the second method, only five cards are initially dealt out. The replacement draw cards are sequentially dealt out from the deck for each discarded card only when the player presses the DRAW button. This method, which is more similar to the way table poker is dealt, is used in the newer machines. The two methods are simply programming variations; from a probability standpoint, they are identical.

VIDEO POKER HANDS

Earlier, in the section on draw poker, the traditional poker hands were listed and described. Although the winning hands in video poker are similar, there are some deviations. For instance, in table poker, in a game with wild cards, five-of-a-kind is the highest-value hand.

In the vast majority of wild-card video poker games, however, five-of-a-kind is a lower-value hand than a royal flush. At the risk of redundancy, following are the most common paying hands in video poker, along with the approximate odds of making the hand after the draw:

Royal Flush:

An ace-high straight flush with no wild cards. Also called a *natural royal*. For most payout schedules, a royal flush will occur once in 40,000 to 45,000 hands, or a little more often if you sacrifice pat hands to draw to a royal. The cards may appear on the video screen in any order, as below.

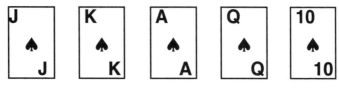

Don't be discouraged if you can't seem to get a royal flush; at 40,000 to 1, it can be a long time in coming. One day at the Plaza, a lady sitting next to me hit a royal flush, so I glibly muttered, "Guess this is your lucky day." She turned to me and snapped, "And it's about time!"

Sequential Royal:

This is a royal flush in which the five cards must appear in ordered sequence on the video screen, as below.

Some machines require the sequence to be right-to-left (as in the above illustration) while others require it to be left-to-right with the Ace at the right end. Using perfect playing strategy, you will make a sequential royal an average of once in 4- to 5-million hands, so don't hold your breath. An even tougher variation is when the sequential royal has to be in a specific suit, which multiplies the odds by four.

Reversible Royal:

Same as the sequential royal except that the sequence can be in either direction, reducing the odds to one in 2+ million. Don't hold your breath for this one, either.

Suited Royal:

A royal flush of a particular designated suit. If you don't change strategy, this hand occurs one-quarter as often as a regular royal flush, or about once in every 160,000 hands. If the strategy favors the specified suit, then it occurs a little more often. The following royal flush would be a *suited* royal if diamonds were specified as the designated suit.

Joker Royal or Deuce Royal:

A royal flush with wild cards. In a joker-wild game, the odds of making it are about one in 12,000. In a deuces-wild game, the odds are about one in

600. The cards may appear on the video screen in any order, as below.

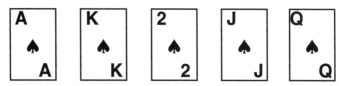

Five-of-a-Kind:

Five cards of the same rank, sometimes called quints. Except for the games of *Five Deck Poker* and *Five Deck Frenzy* (see next chapter), this hand necessarily includes at least one wild card, since a standard deck has only four cards of a given rank, one of each suit.

In some joker-wild games, this is the top-paying hand and will occur once in about 11,000 hands; in deuces wild, the odds are one in 300 hands. In deuces and joker wild games, the top-paying hand is five wild cards, which occurs about once in 130,000 hands.

Five Deck Frenzy has no wild cards, so the top-paying hand is five aces of spades with odds of one chance in almost 15 million.

Straight Flush:

Five consecutive cards, all of the same suit. When the ace is part of the sequence, it is always low; if it is high, the result is a royal flush. A natural straight flush is typically made about once in 9,000 hands. This improves to once in 1700 hands with a joker, and once in 200 hands with deuces wild.

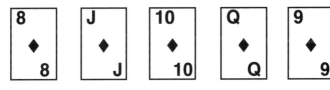

Four-of-a-Kind:

Four cards of the same rank, also called quads. The fifth card is unrelated. Quads can be made an average of about once in every 425 hands. In joker poker, the odds drop to one in 120, and the four wild cards in deuces wild drop the odds to once in every 16 hands.

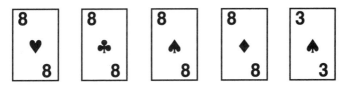

Since quads is a pat hand in a jacks-or-better game, the conventional wisdom is not to draw the fifth card since there is no way to improve. However, not drawing a card to four-of-a-kind is a bad habit to get into. If you play both wild-card and jacks-or-better games you might, without thinking, not draw when you are playing with wild cards and miss a potential five-of-a-kind.

Four-of-a-Kind (Aces):

When four-of-a-kind is limited to a specified rank, it is usually aces, but may also be kings, queens, or deuces. A high payout for four deuces is typically found in deuces wild games. The odds of making four-of-a-kind of a specified rank is one in 5,000.

Four-of-a-Kind (Faces):

When four-of-a-kind is limited to three specified ranks, it is often the face cards (jacks, queens, and kings), but more often twos, threes, and fours, as a group. The odds are about one in 2,000.

Full House:

Three-of-a-kind and a pair. With no wild cards, a full house occurs once in every 90 hands. In joker poker, the odds are one in 65, and in deuces wild, the odds are one in 40.

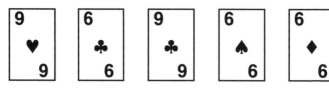

Flush:

Five cards of the same suit. This hand is made as often as a full house— once in every 90 hands. Joker poker is also the same—one in 65. But in deuces wild, the best strategy is to go for straight flushes so the odds of ending up with a flush worsens to one in 60.

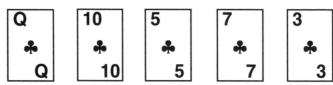

Straight:

Five consecutive cards of mixed suits. Straights occur about as often as full houses and flushes in non-wild and joker poker games. In deuces wild, however, the chances of making a straight improves dramatically to one in 18.

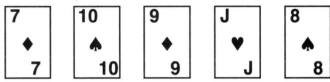

Three-of-a-Kind:

Three cards of the same rank. The remaining two cards are unrelated. The chances of ending up with trips is about one in 14 hands. In joker poker, it is one in eight, and in deuces wild, it is one in four. Three-of-a-kind is the lowest-paying hand in deuces wild.

Two Pairs:

A pair of one rank and a pair of another rank. The fifth card is unrelated. Two pairs win one out of eight hands in non-wild and joker poker games. This is not a paying hand in deuces wild, and is the lowest-paying hand in many joker poker schedules.

Jacks or Better:

Two cards of the same rank. They must be either jacks, queens, kings, or aces. The three remaining cards are unrelated. A pair of jacks or better wins about every five hands. In non-wild games, this is usually the lowest-paying hand. In some games, however, the lowest paying hand may be tens or better, kings or better, or a pair of aces.

CHOOSING THE BEST MACHINE

The average amount of money that a video poker machine returns to the player after a long period of play is called the *payback*. The payback is usually stated as a percentage of the amount that the player invested in the

machine. If, for example, the payback of a game is 101%, then, over the long term, you can expect to make a one percent profit on the money you risked. If the payback is 99%, you can expect to sustain a one percent loss.

THE HOUSE PERCENTAGE

The payback of the game also determines the average profit made by the casino, which is called the *house percentage*. For a payback of, say, 98%, every $100 put into the machine will return a long-term average of $98 to the player.

The remaining $2 is the casino's profit. Actually, the $98 is an *expectation*. It could be more and it could be less. It is the amount that, statistically-speaking, is *expected* to be returned in the form of winnings over a very long period of time. Over the short term, however, anything can happen.

For any given machine, there are two payback numbers. One is the maximum payback for perfect play. This is the payback in which we are interested. It is the highest possible return when the best playing strategy is used, and is the one we have in mind whenever the term "payback" is used in this book. To the casino, this payback has only academic interest because it does not directly define the casino's profit.

The other payback is based on the actual recorded return from the machine. It is the one that the casino cares about because it is an estimate of the casino's potential long-term profit on that machine. Since most players do not apply the best strategy or bet the maximum coins, the payback for those players is typically two to four percent lower than the payback for perfect play. Thus, if the maximum attainable payback on a machine is 99%, the actual recorded payback will typically be about 96%, leaving the casino with a four percent profit.

COIN MULTIPLIERS

All video poker machines employ *coin multipliers*. Most machines will accept one through five coins (or credits) for each hand played. The more coins deposited, the higher the payout for each winning hand. The payouts increase proportionately to the number of coins or credits, except that the largest jackpot is significantly higher when five coins are played. Coin multipliers are designed to encourage players to bet the maximum number of coins.

For most winning hands, the payout for five coins is five times the payout for one coin. For the top hand, however, the jackpot payout for five coins is typically 16 to 20 times the payout for one coin. As a result, when fewer than the maximum number of coins is bet, the average long-term payback percentage is reduced by 1-2%. For this reason, almost all the strategies presented in this book are based on five-coin play. The only exception is for the Second Chance machines described below.

Every so often greediness rears its ugly head, and new video poker machines that accept more than five coins are introduced. Since you have to deposit the maximum number of coins to qualify for the main jackpot, playing them effectively requires a larger bankroll. Most astute players avoid them, so these machines are relatively rare and will continue to be. Because they do not have attractive payout schedules, this book does not mention them any further.

DETAILS OF THE GAMES

Even within a single casino, you will find a bewildering array of different kinds of video poker machines. One way to sort them out is to group them into major categories. Many players come to prefer certain types of machines, which is fine so long as they seek out the best paying machines within that type. Although new kinds of video poker machines regularly appear in the casinos, the following are the major ones to be found today:

NON-PROGRESSIVE MACHINES

Original Jacks or Better

This was the initial form of video poker and is still very popular today. The lowest paying hand is a pair of jacks, and there are no wild cards. The payout schedule is based on standard poker hands and, except for a royal flush, the rank of the cards in a given hand are immaterial. That is, four deuces are worth the same as four queens, and a king-high straight is worth the same as a five-high straight. These machines come in a variety of paybacks from fair (95-96%) to good (97-98%) to excellent (99-100%). Use the charts in the Payout Schedules chapter to help you find the best payers.

Tens or Better

This is basically the same as jacks or better except that the lowest paying hand is a pair of tens. Some tens-or-better machines have excellent paybacks (99%), if you can find one of them. Most, however, pay poorly (92%). They were installed some years ago when the competition for video poker players first became important. They never attained much popularity, so there aren't many around anymore.

Two Pairs or Better

The name tells the tale. The lowest paying hand is two pairs. The best of these machines has a pretty good payback of 98%, but there are also versions that pay only 94%. You will often find two-pairs machines scattered among the jacks-or-better machines; the casinos take advantage of the fact that some players don't seem to know the difference.

Bonus Quads

Bonus machines are basically jacks-or-better machines that offer bonus payouts for specified four-of-a-kind (quad) hands. These non-progressive machines, including double, double-double, and triple bonus varieties, have extra-high payouts for certain quads such as four aces, four face cards, four eights, etc. To compensate for these bonuses, the payouts on some standard hands are somewhat reduced and, in one case, the lowest payout is changed from jacks-or-better to kings-or-better.

As a group, these are the best paying machines in Nevada with paybacks in the range of 99-100%. As a result, they have become the most popular types of video poker machines around. The versions found in Atlantic City and along the Mississippi, however, only pay about 94-98%.

Bonus Royals

This is a small category of non-progressive bonus machines that, instead of quads, have extra-high payouts for certain royal flushes. Most of these games pay back in the range of 99-100%, but depend on some jackpot combinations that occur very rarely, such as a sequential royal flush. The machines we defined for this category are non-progressives. The Progressive Jackpot category (see below) contains many similar games that are designed to build the jackpot value as high as possible before someone wins it.

Joker Wild

This game uses a 53-card deck in which the joker is a wild card. The joker can be substituted for any other card in the deck. In most cases, a royal flush with a joker (called a Joker Royal) does not pay as well as a natural. Many players are attracted to joker poker, despite the fact that in many versions of the game the payback is only fair. Although there are a few machines out there that pay as high as 101%, most of them pay in the range of 94-97%.

Deuces Wild

As the name suggests, in this game all four deuces are wild cards. In all cases, a royal flush with deuces (called a Deuce Royal) pays much less than a natural because it is (typically) 80 times easier to make. All other hands, however, pay the same with or without deuces. Even though the lowest-paying hand is three-of-a-kind, many versions of deuces wild have an excellent payback of 99-101%. Be sure to check the charts in the Payout Schedules chapter because some machines pay only 94-96%.

Deuces and Joker Wild

Five wild cards in a 53-card deck results in a very lively game with over half the hands being potential winners, although they are mostly pushes. If you can find one, the deuces and joker wild machines have an excellent 99% payback in Nevada casinos, but the versions found along the Mississippi pay only about 93%.

Double Joker

Two wild jokers in a 54-card deck, with two pairs being the lowest-paying hand. So far, this game has only been available in Atlantic City. There are two almost identical versions: one has an excellent payback of 100%, the other pays less than 98%. To tell which is which, look them up in the Payout Schedules chapter.

Five Deck Poker

This unique type of video poker game uses five separate decks of cards, one for each card position. Each of the five cards in the original deal comes from its own dedicated, randomly-shuffled 52-card deck.

On the draw, each replacement card is dealt from the same deck as was the original card in that position. As a result, it is possible to have a hand with five identical cards, such as five queens of diamonds. The strategy for *Five Deck Poker* is significantly different than for any other video poker variant.

The top-paying hand is five-of-a-kind, all of the same suit, which pays 10,000 coins for a five-coin bet. The payback for most schedules, however, is only fair to good (95-97%).

PROGRESSIVE MACHINES

Progressive Jackpot

A progressive jackpot network is a group of machines that are electrically connected to a common jackpot pool. As people play the machines, a small percentage of the money paid in by the players is diverted to the jackpot pool, which continues to grow until someone wins it. The jackpot is then reset to a predetermined minimum value and the growth cycle repeats itself.

Each player is competing against the other players on that network, and each time coins are inserted, the jackpot gets a little larger.

A progressive network may consist of a bank of a dozen machines with a jackpot that rarely exceeds a few thousand dollars. The winning progressive hand is usually a natural royal flush, so the chance of hitting the jackpot in such a small localized network is not unreasonable. Local banks of progressive machines can be found for many varieties of games including original jacks or better, bonus quads, bonus royals, deuces wild, and joker wild.

If the machine is part of a city-wide or state-wide network that interconnects hundreds of other machines, the winning progressive hand is always a very rare combination such as a sequential royal flush. Consequently, the jackpot pool can reach lifestyle-altering levels. The chance of winning that jackpot is almost as small as the chance of winning the Power Ball lottery.

Many progressive players do not care about the overall payback of the machine, since they are only really interested in the main jackpot. Until the jackpot gets quite high, the long-term payback for wide-area network games is only fair—and the short-term payback is never very good. Because of their rarity, including sequential royal flushes in the calculations is misleading for the average player.

Consequently, for schedules with jackpot hands that have an expected occurrence of less than 1 in 500,000, two payback percentages are shown in the Payout Schedules chapter, one of which does not take into account the rare hands.

Five Deck Frenzy

This is the progressive version of *Five Deck Poker*. All *Five Deck Frenzy* machines are connected to a wide-area progressive jackpot network, so the payback varies from 98% to well over 100%, depending on the value of the jackpot. The winning progressive jackpot hand is five aces of spades. Because of the low probability of getting that hand (one in almost 15 million), the jackpot can get very large before someone hits it.

DOUBLE DOWN STUD

Double-down stud is not another version of draw poker, but is loosely based on the game of five-card stud poker. Since double-down stud requires little skill and has a simple playing strategy, it will be fully covered in this section. This game has not really caught on, probably because the long-term average payback is less than 98%.

You begin playing by inserting one to ten coins—the tenth coin doubles the payout for a royal flush.

Four cards are dealt face up, and you are given the option of doubling your original bet before the fifth card is dealt. When you make your choice, the fifth card is exposed and the machine pays in accordance with the chart on the following page.

If you insert ten coins, the payout for a royal flush is increased to 2000 per coin. The best strategy is to double when you have the following:

- Any paying hand, from a pair of sixes on up.
- A possible royal flush.
- A possible straight flush.
- A possible flush.
- A possible straight (open-ended).

Do not double on a pair smaller than a six. Do not double an inside or single-ended straight. Remember, this is not draw poker so you do not get to discard any unwanted cards. You just get to see the fifth card after making the doubling decision. This game is only described here in the interest of completeness. It is not recommended, but you may want to try it as a diversion from the draw poker games.

Double Down Stud - Fifth Card Payout Schedule

Winning Hand	1 Coin	10 Coins
Royal Flush	1,000	20,000
Straight Flush	200	2000
Four-of-a-Kind	50	500
Full House	12	120
Flush	9	90
Straight	6	60
Three of a Kind	4	40
Two Pairs	3	30
Jacks or Better	2	20
Sixes-Tens	1	10

NOVELTIES AND ODDITIES

Many video poker machines contain stratagems to help you lose your money a little faster. Some of these ploys kick in after your final hand is displayed and give you another opportunity to win or to lose what you have already won. Although most of them have no effect on the basic playing strategy, we will describe each one so you can decide whether or not you want to play along.

Triple Play

This is an interesting variant in that it isn't quite what it appears to be. The player is dealt three hands at once from three different decks, but only one hand is exposed. The exposed hand is played in a normal manner and when the draw occurs, the same cards that were held appear in the other two hands. Each of the three hands then gets replacement cards dealt from its respective deck. Thus, if you start off with a good hand, you will have three good hands, but if you have a bad hand, you will have three bad hands.

From the standpoint of mathematical probability, this is exactly like playing three different machines simultaneously. The fact that the three hands always have the same held cards somehow adds an exciting flavor. This is a multi-game machine from which the player may select one of several standard versions of bonus quads or deuces wild. To get all three hands dealt, three coins must be deposited; thus, to qualify for the maximum jackpot payout, 15 coins must be deposited—5 for each hand. This accounts for the popularity of the nickel version.

This concept has been expanded to five-play and ten-play versions, which are identical to Triple Play except that up to five hands (or ten hands) are dealt from five (or ten) separate 52-card decks.

Recently, the multi-hand concept was taken about as far as it could go when 50-play and 100-play machines began appearing in some casinos. If you play only 50 hands on a quarter machine, at five coins per hand it would cost you $62.50 per game. Not a problem if you get a good hand. If you get a garbage hand, however, you will have 50 garbage hands, and this will do serious damage to that hundred dollar bill you fed into the bill acceptor.

Double or Nothing

On some video poker machines, whenever you get a winning hand, you are given the option of risking the entire payout on a double-or-nothing bet. If you press the YES button, five new cards appear on the screen, four down and one up. You may then select one of the four face-down cards. If it is higher than the first face-up card, the payout is doubled; if it is lower, you lose your winnings and the game is concluded. A tie is a push, and is replayed. You may continue the doubling-up game as many times as you wish—until you lose.

Although this turns out to be a very fair 1:1 proposition, we don't recommend it. Statistically, the probability of losing is cumulative, so that if you try to double more than one time in succession, your *overall* chances of winning rapidly decrease. On the first try, the chance of winning is 50%, on the second it is 25%, on the third it is 12.5%, and so on. Like any repeated double-or-nothing proposition, you will eventually lose your money.

Double Card

Some jacks-or-better video poker machines deal from a 53-card deck where the extra card is a *double* card. No, it is not a wild card. When it appears in a winning hand, it doubles the payout. Although at first glance it seems like a good deal, whenever the double card appears, it effectively reduces your five-card hand to a four-card hand. It actually interferes with any winning hand that requires five cards such as a straight, flush, or royal flush. If you get a four-straight or a four-flush and the fifth card is a double, you should discard the double. Better yet, you should discard this game.

Second Chance

On some video poker machines, you are given the option of taking a sixth card whenever your final hand, after the draw, is one that could be improved to a straight or better. The sixth card is dealt from the remaining cards in the same randomly-shuffled deck that was used for the original hand. A new payout schedule appears on the screen showing the possible winning hands for that particular situation. For instance, if your final hand is two pairs, the new schedule will show a payout for a possible full house. This payout is not necessarily the same as the original payout schedule, but is set so that the overall payback with the sixth card is about 97%, which is usually less than the overall payback of the machine.

If, after the draw, you have a possible straight or better, the back of a sixth card will appear on the screen and the SECOND CHANCE button will illuminate. To accept the option, press the button. You may now insert one to five additional coins (or credits), regardless of how many coins you originally bet. The machine will expose the sixth card and automatically select the best five out of the six cards

The main advantage to second chance is that you can change the value of your bet in midstream. Therefore, the best initial approach is to play one coin at a time and use the recommended strategy for the posted payout schedule. Only activate the second chance option if you draw four cards to a royal. Then insert five coins (or credits) to maximize the jackpot and go for the sixth card.

Progressive Second Chance

This is another version of second chance that has a separate progressive jackpot for royal flushes. The option kicks in when you have four cards to a royal flush. It can raise the overall payback of the machine to well over 100%, even when the jackpot is at its lowest level. You are allowed to drop in five coins, even if your original bet was only a single coin. Be sure to do that. Progressive Second Chance is definitely a worthwhile gamble.

PLAYING THE BEST STRATEGY

After the initial five cards are dealt out, it is up to the player to decide which cards to hold and which to discard. This decision is the only control exercised by the player and is a significant factor in the outcome of the

> **ESSENTIAL!**
> To win at video poker, you must learn and play the correct strategies as shown in this chapter. Stick to the strategies and always play the full five coins.

game. Therefore, it is important to apply the correct playing strategy when making the hold/discard decision.

STRATEGY METHODS

There are two basic approaches to video poker strategy. The first is the intuitive, or seat-of-the-pants, method which forfeits one to two percent of the possible payback due to inaccuracy. This method is advanced by several books and is used by most players. It does avoid the principal strategy pitfalls (such as being complex and hard to memorize), but misses many of the subtleties. Its major advantage is simplicity.

The other method is mathematical. It is based on detailed probability calculations and is, therefore, exact. Although the mathematical method is far more complicated, it results in a perfect strategy that is 100% correct. Its major disadvantage is complexity.

This book starts with the perfect mathematical strategy but simplifies the application of it, with minimal loss in accuracy, so that it is almost as easy to use as the intuitive method.

There are many good descriptions of the perfect mathematical strategy for drawing cards in video poker, but most of them over-complicate the problem. For instance, a portion of the strategy for jacks-or-better is often given as:

4-Card Outside Straight Flush	**Draw 1 card**
Two Pairs	**Draw 1 card**
4-Card Inside Straight Flush	**Draw 1 card**

What this means is that drawing to an outside straight flush is preferential to drawing to two pairs, and that drawing to two pairs is preferential to drawing to an inside straight flush. This strategy is absolutely correct. However, a possible straight flush and two pairs cannot occur in the same hand, so the strategy can be simplified by saying:

4-Card Straight Flush	**Draw 1 card**
Two Pairs	**Draw 1 card**

This is mathematically identical to the more complicated version. In fact, one can also say:

Two Pairs	**Draw 1 card**
4-Card Straight Flush	**Draw 1 card**

Since both hands are mutually exclusive, it doesn't matter in what order they are listed in the strategy table. This is typical of the simplifications used in the Playing Strategy Tables chapter.

Some lines in strategy tables have modifiers, and are not always easy to interpret properly. Wherever possible, such lines are interpreted for you. Take, for example, the following line:

4-Card Outside Straight (2 high cards)

Because of the modifier *(2 high cards)*, it takes a moment or two to figure out. In the Playing Strategy Tables chapter, that strategy line is given as:

9-10-J-Q (mixed suits)

...which means exactly the same, but is immediately clear to the player and can be directly matched to the hand on the video screen.

Another example is:

3-Card Royal Flush (queen high)

...which is not hard to understand.

The following line is still easier to see and can be matched up more quickly and accurately to the screen image:

```
10-J-Q (same suit)
```

In every case where a wordy strategy line defines only a single hand, the Playing Strategy Tables chapter will, instead, show the actual cards in the hand. Wherever practical, this is also done when the line defines two or three different hands. Of course, for a line without a modifier, such as: *3-Card Straight Flush*, there are too many possible hands to do this. Besides, without a modifier, the line is easy to interpret.

Simplification was sometimes attained by rounding to the second decimal place in the probability calculations for some of the dealt hands. When compared with most published strategies that are based on very precise numbers, the difference in real-world play turns out to be negligible.

To apply the mathematical strategy with absolute accuracy takes considerable concentration, which is simply not possible for most people. With all the distractions in a typical casino, trying to use a complicated strategy can easily result in inadvertent playing errors that reduce the overall payback. If that happens, you are probably just as well off using the intuitive method. The simplified strategy presented in the Playing Strategy Tables chapter will reduce such errors and result in coming closer to the maximum theoretical payback for the machine being played.

BASIC STRATEGY RULES

To assure that you are getting the highest return from a video poker machine, a certain amount of playing discipline must be used. The following basic rules have to be followed to assure that the best strategy is effectively applied:

Play the Maximum Coins

Last year, while waiting for somebody at the Stratosphere, I was idly playing a jacks or better machine, one quarter at a time. When my friend showed up, the machine had five credits showing, so I hit the PLAY 5 CREDITS button, just to be done with it. To my amazement, I was dealt three cards to a spade royal and made it on the draw. The payout was 4000 coins ($1000), or the equivalent of 800 coins per quarter. Had I continued to play one quarter at a time, the payout would have been only 250 coins, or a measly $62.50. The moral to this story is to play the maximum coins (usually five), unless you have a good reason not to.

The one consistency in all video poker machines is that the per-coin payout for the highest hand is always enhanced when the maximum number of coins (or credits) is played. Although there are situations where single-coin play is advisable (such as Second Chance machines), the playing strategies in this book are based on five-coin play, unless otherwise noted.

Many recreational players find that dollar machines deplete their bankroll too quickly. Therefore, if you feel uneasy playing for $5 a hand, move to a quarter machine. If you insist on playing fewer than the maximum coins, be aware that the long-term payback will be reduced by 1-2%—and much more if you hit an early royal, as I did. However, there is one caution: If you move from a quarter machine to a nickel machine, be sure that the payout schedule is the same.

Although there isn't much variation in schedules between quarter, dollar, and five-dollar machines, most nickel machines have significantly poorer payout schedules.

Never Hold a Kicker

A kicker is an unmatched card held in the hand when drawing replacement cards. Some video poker players hate to discard an ace, even if keeping it doesn't improve their hand. This is a throwback to the table game where such strategy is sometimes appropriate. In video poker, however, holding a kicker is disastrous because it significantly reduces the chances of improving a hand.

For instance, on a full-pay jacks-or-better machine, keeping a kicker with a high pair reduces the overall payback by over 1.5%. If you are dealt a low pair, discarding two instead of three cards reduces the payback by almost four percent. Don't do it.

Stick to the Strategy

Do not try to outguess the strategy table. The table is based on mathematical probabilities and your hunch is not. Once in a while you may guess correctly, but over the long run the strategy table will serve you well. If you don't like the idea of breaking a straight or a flush in order to draw one card to a possible royal, maybe you are playing the wrong game.

Do not depend on your memory

Take this book into the casino and refer to it frequently. Many of the differences between the payout charts and the strategy tables are quite subtle. Until you are familiar with a particular version of video poker don't depend too much on your memory.

For instance, if you are not absolutely sure what to do when your hand contains four cards to a flush along with a pair of kings, be sure to open the book. After you have played a particular game for a while, you will get to know the strategy by heart.

Quit when you are ahead

This rule actually falls in the category of money management, but it is so important that it should be a part of the overall playing strategy. When you hit a jackpot or a good bonus payout, that is a good time to quit for a while. Experience has shown that with continued play, the chances are that you will fritter away the winnings, and that is what the casinos depend on.

Do some people actually quit after hitting a jackpot or a nice bonus payout? You bet they do. To illustrate: Fitzgeralds in downtown Las Vegas had a bank of five bonus quads machines called *Double Bonus Poker*, with a sign above them that said *Certified Loose 100.2% Payback*. The actual payback on these machines was just a little bit more than 100.1%, but casino puffery, being what it is, rounded the number up rather than down.

Anyway, one day I was playing one of them when someone stepped up to the machine next to mine and dropped in five quarters. Curiosity, being what it is, I glanced to the side and noticed that this person was wearing ordinary business clothes and appeared to be a local, rather than a tourist.

Before I looked back to my own machine, I also noticed that he was dealt a pair of aces. A moment later, I heard a heavy clatter of coins and realized that he had won and cashed out.

As soon as he scooped out the quarters and walked away, I looked at the screen again and saw four aces. The payout was 160 coins for each coin bet for a total of $200. This person clearly knew that if he continued playing, the machine would probably get all or most of that $200 back. Smart fellow.

THE LONG AND THE SHORT OF IT

Long-Term Payback

It should be recognized that the application of the best strategies given in this book, or any other book, doesn't guarantee a net gain for the player. To understand why, it is necessary to grasp the meaning of long-term payback as applied to a video poker machine.

If the stated payback of a machine is 101%, then, *over the long term*, you can expect to make a one percent profit on the money you risked. If the payback is 99%, then, *over the long term*, you can expect to sustain a one percent loss. Except for the phrase:

"over the long term," this is an easy concept to understand. But, we need to define what is meant by *long term.*

In almost all jacks or better, deuces wild, and joker wild games, the highest paying hand is a royal flush. The probability of making a royal flush is roughly one in 40,000. Therefore, in order to attain the long-term payback percentage, it is necessary to hit a royal flush an average of once in every 40,000 hands. But, you say, it would take me forever to play 40,000 hands, even if I had a sufficient bankroll. There's the rub!

It actually gets worse than that. The Poisson distribution is a mathematical tool used by statisticians for analyzing rare events that randomly occur over a period of time. Applying the Poisson distribution to video poker, we find that in the course of playing 40,000 hands, there is only a 63% chance of getting at least one royal flush. The worrisome part is that there is a 37% chance of getting *no* royal flushes in 40,000 hands. This means that even if you play 40,000 hands, there is no guarantee that you will get a royal flush.

In fact, until you get your first royal flush, your average percentage return will gradually slip lower and lower. It will spike up whenever you hit an occasional quad or straight flush, and then resume its downward trend. When you finally get that elusive royal, you will usually recoup all your losses and even jump ahead. The key in all this is the word *average.* Although the average recurrence of a royal flush is every 40,000 hands, you might get your first royal after playing only 100 hands, or you might have to play 100,000 hands. That's why they call it gambling!

So what *is* the long term? For one, it depends on the game. In most non-progressive games, there is about a 95% statistical probability of hitting at least one royal flush in 120,000 hands. Most professional gamblers, however, feel more comfortable using a "five times average" rule of thumb, which works out to 200,000 hands (40,000 x 5). The comfort factor is understandable, since in 200,000 hands, the statistical probability of getting at least one royal flush is better than 99%.

In progressive games, the jackpot hand is often a sequential royal flush. The probability of hitting a sequential is one chance in almost 5 million, in which case the long term would be close to 25 million hands. I don't think you can do that—even over an extended vacation. Getting five aces of spades in Five Deck Frenzy is even more remote—one chance in 15 million.

Short-Term Payback

The only people who should be concerned with long-term payback are the professionals and the casinos. To the rest of us, it doesn't have much meaning because all of our playing is over relatively short periods of time.

Then why are all our payback numbers based on the long-term expectation? Statistically, *long term* means that the number of hands approaches infinity and, as such, has become the defacto standard and uniform way of stating the payback.

Providing short-term payback percentages seems

like a good idea except that it gets too complicated. For one, we don't always know what short term means. Is it 100 hands, 1000 hands, or 10,000 hands? Not only does the defined number of hands affect the payback percentage, but then what strategy should be used? The short-term payback does go up a little if we don't break pat hands to go for a royal. But, one of the exciting things about video poker is getting a royal flush. If we change the strategy, we may miss a royal—and few of us want to do that, even if the average payback is half a point better.

Obviously, this situation is in need of some relief. To show short-term paybacks on each individual payout schedule in the Payout Schedules chapter would be too cumbersome. Instead, in the Short-Term Correction Tables chapter, they are shown as corrections to the long-term paybacks in the Payout Schedules chapter. Each Short-Term Correction table shows the downward correction that should be applied to the long-term payback percentage, depending on the number of hands played in a short-term session. You can still use the long-term payback numbers in the Payout Schedules chapter as a comparison for deciding which games to play. The Short-Term Correction tables will simply give you a dose of reality.

The good news is that when you are figuring the number of hands in the Short-Term Correction tables, you can combine all your short playing sessions to make a long one. Like the little white ball in roulette or the dice in craps, the random number generator in a legal video poker machine does not have a memory. Each hand is from a random deal and is independent of previous events. This means that four one-hour sessions at four different machines is statistically the same as one four-hour session on one machine.

Let's say you are in Las Vegas for three days and you play the video poker machines about eight hours a day. If you average 400 hands an hour, which is a normal rate, then your three-day-long session would be:

**400 hands per hour x 8 hours x 3 days
= 9600 hands**

This is almost 10,000 hands. Thus, when you look in the Short-Term Correction chapter to get an idea of your short-term payback, you can see that the reduction in long-term payback is about 1.5%, no matter which machine you play. If you played 25,000 hands, the correction drops to about 0.7%.

For another dose of reality, the wide-area progressive games in the Payout Schedules chapter list two different payback percentages. One of them is the standard long-term payback. The other payback percentage disregards rare hands such as sequential royals and five aces of spades. Except for Five Deck Frenzy, the difference between the two payback numbers is only about 0.3%.

In Five Deck Frenzy, disregarding the five spade aces reduces the payback by about one percent. To be realistic, you should only think about the lower payback, and if you get lucky and hit the progressive jackpot, consider it an unexpected windfall.

HOW TO USE THE CHARTS IN THIS BOOK

Selecting the Best Machine

The Payout Schedules chapter contains charts detailing the payout schedules of the most common video poker games found in the major casinos. The charts are organized by category so that the player can more easily match the correct chart to a particular game. When examining a video poker machine in a casino, first determine the kind of game (Original Jacks or Better, Bonus Quads, Deuces Wild, etc.) and then flip through Chapter 7 until you find that category. As a double check that you are in the right section, the first page lists typical descriptive names.

In the larger sections, the charts are sorted in a specific logical order to make them easier to locate. For example, in the Bonus Quads section, the charts are in order of the highest quad payout. This is explained on the introductory page for each section. When you are in the right section, compare the payout schedule of the game to the payout charts shown. Once the correct schedule chart is found—which should take only a few seconds— it will show the long-term payback percentage and the strategy code.

For simplicity, the payout charts in this book show only the one-coin and five-coin columns. If, for some reason you need to, the two-, three-, and four-coin columns are easy to derive; they are simply multiples of the one-coin column. Payback percentages are for perfect strategy and 5-coin play.

Finally, a few of the low-paying schedules show a strategy notation of "NR" (for *not recommended*) and have no associated strategy chart. These schedules are included for reference purposes—to help you recognize a poor paying machine when you see it. If that is the only kind of machine you can find in your area, you will be better off playing a different game.

Applying the Playing Strategy

After finding the matching payout chart in the Payout Schedules chapter, note the strategy code and turn to the indicated strategy table in the Playing Strategy Tables chapter. Each strategy table lists all possible hands in the order they should be played. After the initial five cards are dealt, work your way down from the top of the strategy table until you find a match and then draw the indicated number of cards.

You do not have to consult the strategy table for every hand that is dealt. For most hands, the correct strategy is obvious. The main purpose of the table is to resolve conflicts when there is more than one way to logically play a hand. For instance, what do you do if you are dealt a pat flush that includes a four-card royal? What about a four-flush that includes a three-card royal? And once you have learned these things, remember to recheck the strategy table whenever you play a new type of game.

Those Puzzling Hands

When you examine the strategy tables, there are some dealt hands that may be somewhat puzzling—

especially if you are not a statistician. This is chiefly because the value of every dealt hand in the strategy tables is based on the sum total of all the possible paying hands that can occur after the draw. Many times, the probability of filling the obvious hand is very low, so the actual value of the holding is mainly based on lesser paying hands that occur more frequently. To help you suppress the desire to modify such strategies, we will endeavor to explain their rationale in non-mathematical terms.

In Jacks or Better (and Bonus Quads), you will often see a dealt hand in the strategy listing that says *2-Card Royal (no ten)*, such as the hand shown below.

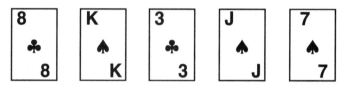

You may wonder why "(no ten)" is specified for this hand. The chance of drawing a royal flush to the two held cards is very small, so the net value in the holding is mainly based on drawing a pair of jacks or better. If one of the two held cards is a ten instead of a jack or better, the probability of drawing a high pair is cut in half.

The same reasoning applies to the holding *4-Card Inside Straight (3 HC)*, which is an inside (or single-ended) straight with three high cards.

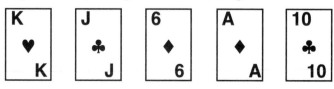

The three high cards are important because of the improved chance of making a jacks-or-better hand. In the above hand, there are only four cards (queens) remaining in the undealt portion of the deck that will fill the inside straight, whereas there are nine cards (3 jacks + 3 kings + 3 aces) that will make jacks or better. If the 4-card inside straight has only two high cards, you are better off drawing to the high cards alone.

Finally, another puzzling line that appears near the bottom of many strategy tables is *3 High Cards (no ace)*. You will not find that strategy line in this book, since it has been restated as *J-Q-K (mixed suits)*. However, you may still wonder about the aversion for aces.

Well, yet another way of stating this line is **3-Card Outside Straight (king high)**. If the ace were allowed, it would become a single-ended straight, which has a much lower probability of being made on the draw—while the chance of making a high pair isn't any better for a holding of Q-K-A than it is for J-Q-K.

DEALING WITH THE CASINO

If you are a recreational video poker player, you should bring this book with you into the casino. It is of little value as a reference if it is lying at home or in your hotel room. You'll need to refer to it whenever you are faced with

UP AND UP?

You can play slots and video poker in Nevada and New Jersey, knowing that the possibility of encountering a rigged machine is almost non-existent.

a tricky draw and your memory lapses, whenever you are trying to figure if a progressive jackpot is high enough to be worth playing, and whenever you want to try a new type of game. Don't leave it behind.

What do casinos think about someone who brings in a book? I don't know about *every* casino, but the dozens and dozens that I have researched (mostly in Las Vegas) would probably pay no attention. How can I be so sure? In doing my research, I wander around the casinos with a clipboard and a notebook. When I find a machine of interest, I stand in front of it and methodically write down all the information on the machine. Then I frequently play the machine to verify its operation or to bring up a particular payout schedule on the screen. I have done these things in plain view of any number of casino employees including maintenance people, floor supervisors, and security guards. No one has ever said anything or paid more than passing attention to me.

One reason the casinos love video machines is that they are pretty foolproof. The only way for a player to cheat is to physically tamper with the equipment. Casino operators have always known that referring to books and notes cannot affect the outcome of a traditional slot machine. Although that is not as true for video poker, most casino personnel include video poker in the same category with traditional slots. The slot mentality was established a long time ago, and it's not about to change now.

However, if you win a large jackpot, I suggest you put the book away before the casino official making the payoff arrives. If, at that time, this book is propped open next to your machine, I really can't predict the reaction.

ARE VIDEO POKER MACHINES HONEST?

The State of Nevada probably has the most effective gaming commission in the world. For that reason alone, I believe all video poker and slot machines in legal casinos in Nevada are honest. Furthermore, the Nevada Gaming Commission is not only effective—it is tough. Almost all the casinos have such a big investment that they cannot take any risks with their gaming licenses. Even a short term suspension would result in an enormous monetary loss.

In Nevada, a new model of video poker or slot machine cannot be installed until it is approved by the Commission. The greatest concern in video poker games is that the virtual playing cards are electronically shuffled and dealt in a totally-random fashion, and the greatest concern in slot machines is that when the spinning reels stop, they display symbols in a totally-random manner. To assure that this happens, Commission technicians carefully evaluate the software algorithm that defines the random number generator and make sure that the machine has no secondary programming. Secondary programming, a nice term for rigging, is anything that changes the randomness of the outcome of the machine.

For example, a simple software change could make a royal flush occur a little less often than predicted by the laws of probability.

The technicians also physically test the machine to demonstrate that it consistently deals the cards randomly and pays in accordance with the posted schedule. Furthermore, all casinos are subjected to routine unannounced inspections in which one or more machines may be physically moved to the Gaming Commission laboratory for a teardown inspection and extensive testing.

Basically the same thing can be said about New Jersey, although their gaming inspection procedures do not appear to be as rigorous. The inspectors are mostly concerned that the average long-term payback falls within the statute requirements. They do not care about randomness or secondary programming. Although insiders insist that the machines are fundamentally the same as those approved for use in Nevada—they do not have to be. Because most video poker and slot games in New Jersey have less favorable payout schedules, casino profitability is higher and the pressure to use secondary programming is lower.

Once you leave Nevada and New Jersey, however, the picture gets cloudy. Some of the states that have permitted limited casino gambling, such as Illinois and Louisiana, have also set up gaming commissions. However, the effectiveness of their field inspections is probably quite limited. I wouldn't worry too much in these states because the video poker and slot paybacks are so poor that they don't really need to cheat. But then, greediness knows no limits.

What about legal casinos that are not monitored by anyone or are monitored by an ineffective gaming board?—and there are plenty of these from coast to coast. Some machines exported to other countries contain internal switches allowing the casino operator to adjust the frequency of high-paying hands. There is no reason to believe that such machines are not also used somewhere in this country. The only reasonable advice is: Gambler beware. Finally, you must assume that in any illegal gambling hall the machines are rigged.

The bottom line is that you can play in Nevada with complete confidence that the video poker and slot machines are honest. That is, the deal and draw are from a randomly-shuffled deck, and there is no secondary programming to change the natural probabilities. In New Jersey, you are probably okay unless you are playing in a place that is having financial problems. Elsewhere, there is little or no oversight and you are at the mercy of the casino operators.

ABOUT THE IRS

The relationship between gambling and the IRS is a complex subject that even confounds lawyers and accountants specializing in this area. We do not intend to give you any tax or legal advice, but will only make you aware of certain IRS requirements. It is valuable to know about some of these things before encountering them in a real situation.

If you engage in casino transactions of more than $10,000, you should consult an accountant familiar with gaming laws. Casinos must report all cash transactions in excess of $10,000 to the IRS. They must also report an aggregate of cash transactions that occur within a 24-hour period and total to more than $10,000. If you place a large bet at a sports book, cash in chips, or even cash a check larger than $10,000, it must be reported. This is just a reporting requirement (presumably to control money laundering) and doesn't mean you have to pay taxes on the transaction. The state of Nevada also has a similar reporting requirement.

The IRS rule that is most important to video poker players is the requirement for the casino to report any slot machine (including video poker) jackpot of $1200 or more by submitting a W-2G form.

Such winnings are considered ordinary income by the IRS and must be reported under "Other Income" on your 1040 tax return. You can reduce the tax burden (up to the amount of your winnings) if you can prove that you had offsetting gambling losses in the same year. Such losses cannot be subtracted from itemized winnings, but must be listed separately under "Miscellaneous Deductions." However, you also cannot reduce your overall tax by taking a *net* gambling loss—you can only offset winnings.

How do you prove that you had gambling losses? By keeping a detailed dairy of all your gambling activities. How detailed? The IRS recommendation is that, as a minimum, you record the date, time, and amount of your wins and losses, the type of game, denomination, and serial number of each machine played, the name and location of the casino, and the names of any people (witnesses) with you at the time. Supporting documentation such as airline ticket receipts and hotel bills will help to convince an IRS auditor that you were actually there.

However, unless you are a professional in the business of gambling *and* your trip was primarily for business purposes, do not try to deduct expenses such as transportation, hotel rooms, or restaurants.

Once you get used to the idea, you will see that keeping a diary is not as daunting as it first appears. How you actually deal with it, that is, what you put in and what you leave out, is entirely your decision.

Just keep in mind that if the entire diary does not appear to be reasonable, an auditor may judge that it is inaccurate and disallow it.

You may have wondered why some video poker machines pay 4700 coins (on a five-coin bet) for a royal flush. It is an obvious attempt to push the $1200 reporting rule as far as it will go. On a quarter machine, a 4700-coin jackpot amounts to $1175, which just gets under the wire. Whenever the payout is less than $1200, they hand you the cash and don't even ask your name. How sweet it is!

If you gamble and lose money in the stock market, you can deduct a net loss from your taxable income. If you gamble and lose money in a legal casino, you must pay taxes on any net winnings, but are not permitted to deduct a net gambling loss. This is a one-sided proposition, since it is obvious that the vast majority of recreational gamblers are net losers. How else could the gaming industry have built all those expensive hotels? It is no great wonder that some gamblers try to conceal their meager winnings.

SLOT CLUBS

Most people believe there is no such thing as a free lunch. If you also believe that, then you haven't spent much time in Las Vegas. Slot clubs actually give you more than a free lunch. You can get a free room, a free dinner, and maybe even a free show. Of course, to get these comps you have to play the machines. But then, that's what you are doing anyway, so you might as well cash in. For the slot machine and video poker player, slot clubs have no down side.

Slot clubs operate on the same principle as frequent flier clubs. They are designed to encourage you to gamble in their casino by rewarding serious players with various comps. This is done with a computerized player tracking system that keeps tabs on each player's activity so that the comps can be awarded in a fair and consistent manner.

The best approach is to determine which casinos you prefer, and then join their slot clubs. This is easy to do—it takes only a few moments to fill out a slot-club application. You will also have to show them some form of photo identification to verify your identity. The main purpose of the application is to record your mailing address so they can send discount coupons and information on special promotions. In most casinos you will be given some discounts or comps just for signing up.

After you have signed up, you will be issued a coded card so that the computer can track your playing habits. The more you play, the more points you rack up. These points can then be traded in for a variety of comps. Even if you don't use the card, the casino will mail special offers to entice you to come in and play.

When you play the machines, be sure to always insert your card so that you can accumulate points. Every slot machine and almost every video poker machine has a card reader that accepts slot-club cards. Remember, however, that the card has to be from the casino in which you are playing. When you insert the card, a screen display will greet you by name and tell you how many points you have accrued. When you leave the machine be sure to retrieve your card. If you forget or lose the card, don't worry—you can easily get another.

In fact, most casinos will honor a request for two cards so that you can play two machines at the same time. Furthermore, you and your spouse can combine your accumulated points by setting up a joint account.

If you are a regular player, the comps from most slot clubs will add 0.1-0.5% to the total amount of your wagers, and some as high as 1%. A few casinos even offer cash rebates. These comps and rebates are based on the total *action*, which is much larger than the amount you actually risk. Let's say you start with $20 worth of quarters and play about 400 hands of video poker in an hour.

After just two hours of play at five coins a hand, you have cycled those 80 quarters through the machine 50 times (800 hands x 5 coins ÷ 80 quarters = 50). Whether you came out ahead or lost the entire $20, you generated $1000 worth of action (800 hands at $1.25 a hand = $1000). Many people do not realize how little money has to be at risk to generate those comps. Be sure to take advantage of it.

TIPPING

Let me say at the outset that I don't believe in tipping unless a service has been rendered in an efficient and pleasant manner. In a casino, tipping is never required. You are in total control as to when, where, and how much to tip.

Something many people are unaware of is that if you give someone a large tip for an instance of extraordinary service, your tip will be shared with the other employees in that service group on that shift. To comply with IRS regulations, all tips must be pooled and taxes withheld by the employer before the remaining money is divided among the workers. So your big tip is first taxed and then the balance is split up evenly between all the workers in that group. This doesn't seem to bother some people, but it bothers me.

In a restaurant the tipping situation is well defined. The 15% tip has become so standardized that many patrons leave 15% whether the service was good, bad, or mediocre. In a casino, however, there are large gray areas. So much so that many people overtip when tipping isn't even indicated.

Let's start with the change person. Change persons are not normally tipped for making change. So the conventional wisdom is that if a change person provides a special service, a tip would be appropriate. What sort of special service could you get from a change person? I don't really know. Changing a hundred dollar bill? But that is her job, and changing a hundred is not particularly difficult.

I've read in some books that you should tip a change person who directs you to a "hot" machine. Granted, that *would* be a special service, but how could a change person know which machines are hot—and if she really knows, why aren't her friends playing them? This is probably becoming a moot point, now that almost all machines accept bills.

After winning a jackpot you might tip the change person just because you feel generous. But then, shouldn't you also tip the person that paid you off, and the security guard that accompanied this person? How about the minimum-wage person that cleaned up the coin wrappers and the ash trays around your machine? Should you tip all these people? Remember that you will probably pay taxes on your winnings. Any tips you give out will be pooled and taxed as well.

The other service provider that you encounter while playing video poker is the cocktail waitress. This is a no-brainer. You normally tip her 50¢ to a dollar per drink, depending on her efficiency and the complexity of the drink you order. If you are playing a dollar machine, I suggest you tip at least a dollar or you will look like a cheapskate.

AND, FINALLY...

In the Introduction, I stated that this book would contain no math. If you read all of it, you know that I kept my promise. Oh, sure, the short term payback correction tables contain payback adjustments, but that is just simple arithmetic. The Statistical Tables chapter contains statistical tables showing the odds of getting certain video poker hands. These tables are included for those readers that are interested in such things.

The tables in the Playing Strategy Tables chapter can only be derived using intensive statistical analysis. Of course, most of this is done with the help of a computer, but there is still a lot of drudgery mathematics involved. All you get to see are the results.

The information in this book was kept as simple

and understandable as possible because it was not written to impress professional players or other gambling book writers. Although some professionals can undoubtedly learn a few things from these pages, this book was primarily directed at you, the recreational player. Hopefully, it will help to stretch your bankroll and help you to win a jackpot or two.

Now, go to the Payout Schedules chapter and find the payout chart for your favorite machine. Is the payback percentage lower than you thought it might be? Welcome to the real world of deceptive payout schedules. With the help of this book, you can now go find a machine with a good payback and make it your new favorite.

INTRODUCTION TO SLOTS

The slots scene has changed dramatically during the last twenty-five years. Today, few slot machines resemble the old mechanical "one-arm bandits" of the past. The classic pull-handle on the right side of slot machines is

OVERVIEW

Playing the slots is a lot of fun, and you can make money–but you have to know what you're doing.

So let's get acquainted now with the basics!

rapidly disappearing, as more players prefer the ease and speed of pushing buttons. Not only have the machines been electrified, but most of them are now completely computerized.

The one-coin, one-payline three-reel slot machine has virtually disappeared, having been replaced by multi-coin machines, many of which have three or more paylines. Even these machines are beginning to look old-fashioned as the casino floors are being taken over by flashy progressive machines with entertainment themes and graphics-intensive video slots with special bonus screens.

Many of these newer machines will rapidly eat your bankroll unless you've taken the time to learn how to play them properly. They are no longer the mindless games of the old days when all you needed to do was slip in a coin and yank the handle.

While playing at a video poker machine, you may occasionally look around and notice some very interesting slot machines. These games are carefully designed to attract casual observers, such as yourself, and draw them into their web.

Of course, there is nothing wrong with a video poker player switching to a slot machine for a change of scenery. If you do decide to take a slot break, however, you should be careful that you don't squander your video poker bankroll as a result of uninformed slot playing technique. To keep this from happening, we hereby offer a few chapters on slots, summarizing the most important slot playing information and techniques.

SLOT MACHINE BASICS

For a long time, a slot machine consisted of three side-by-side *reels* that displayed pictures of bells, bars, sevens, and various fruits such as cherries, lemons, and plums. The action was entirely mechanical and, after inserting a coin, the reels were set in motion by pulling down a long handle at the right side. The machine paid off by dropping coins into a tray when certain *symbols* lined up in the window behind the horizontal *payline*.

Those old mechanical slot machines are now considered to be antiques. Although modern slot machines still use the basic principle of spinning reels with symbols on them, they have become very sophisticated computer-controlled devices. Instead of pulling a handle (which is still an option on some machines), most players activate the reels by pushing a button.

Today, almost all slots take multiple coins and have built-in paper currency validators that accept any denomination from $1 to $100. In some of the newest machines, there are as many as six simulated spinning reels displayed on a video screen, using a large variety of different symbols.

RANDOMNESS

New models and styles of slot machines have to obtain approval before they can be installed in those gaming jurisdictions that have effective gaming control. The main concern is that the random number generator (RNG) in each machine is operating properly.

The RNG is one of the chips on the computer board inside the machine. It randomly generates thousands of numbers a second, with each number sequence defining a specific set of symbols. The instant you press the SPIN REELS button, the next set of randomly-generated numbers is selected, and this set of numbers defines the symbol combination that appears on the reels or on the video screen.

As a result, the machine operates in a totally random fashion, and there isn't anything a player can do to change that.

PAYBACK

The average amount of money that a slot machine returns to the player after a long period of play is called the *payback*. The payback is stated as a percentage of the amount that the player invested in the machine. If the payback is 95%, for example, you can expect to lose five percent of every dollar that you play.

By adjusting the number of symbols on the reels and by changing the payoff combinations, a slot machine can be made to pay back any desired percentage. The payback typically ranges from 80% to 99%, except in New Jersey where, by law, slots have to pay back at least 83%.

Slots that are set to the lower end of the range are considered to be *tight*, while those at the upper end are *liberal* or *loose*. Unlike video poker machines, however, there is no clear way to tell which machines are the best. The posted payout schedule on the machine is of little help without knowing how many winning symbols are on the reels, which is information not readily available to the player.

However, there are ways to compensate for this problem, which will be covered later.

A slot machine is considered *hot* when it is paying out more than expected. Conversely, it is considered *cold* when it is paying less than expected. Most machines, regardless of how loose or tight they are to begin with, go through hot cycles and cold cycles. Thus, a hot tight machine is better than a cold loose one. Later on, we will explain how to judge whether a machine is currently running hot or cold.

DENOMINATIONS

The denomination of a slot machine is defined as the smallest amount of money needed to spin the reels. The casinos and the machine manufacturers have taken this about as far as it will go, in that there are machines in all the following denominations on the casino floors:

1¢, 5¢, 10¢, 25¢, 50¢, $1, $2, $5, $25, $100

Yes, there are still penny slot machines out there. The new ones accept paper money and allow you to bet up to 250 coins, so they are quite profitable for the casinos. The advice, however, is to not play them because they tend to be tight. At the other end of the spectrum are the $25 and $100 machines. If you haven't seen one of these, just step into the high-limit slot area of one of the classier casinos. In most casinos, though, the majority of the machines are nickels, quarters, and dollars—quarters being the most popular of all.

With almost all slot machines now accepting paper money and registering credits, it was inevitable that multi-denominational machines would be the next step.

And, sure enough, they have arrived. Some of the first ones offer a choice of 5¢, 10¢, or 25¢, while others offer a choice of 25¢, 50¢, or $1. All the player has to do is insert a bill and then push a button indicating the denomination choice. After that, the machine plays like any other.

MULTIPLE PAYLINES

So far, we have been discussing three-reel single payline slot machines. You surely have noticed that there are plenty of three-reel slots with multiple-paylines on the casino floors. While a single payline slot has one horizontal line across the window, some machines have three or more lines. A three-payline slot has two extra horizontal lines, one above and one below the center line, giving you two additional chances of hitting a winning combination.

Although you may activate one, two, or three of the paylines by inserting one, two, or three coins, to qualify for the maximum jackpot benefit, you must play all three coins.

There are also five-payline slots, where two of the lines are diagonals criss-crossing the window, giving you four additional chances (over a single payline) of winning. These are usually five-coin machines, one for each payline, and here again you must play the maximum number of coins to qualify for the maximum jackpot benefit. From the standpoint of return on investment, the multiple-payline slots are perfectly fine machines if you don't mind the higher bankroll requirement.

Finally, some of the newest bonus slot machines have six reels that are simulated on a video screen, with up to forty paylines that zigzag in almost every direction across the screen. As explained below, to play most video and bonus slot machines effectively requires some experience and specialized knowledge.

INTRODUCTION TO SLOTS

COIN MULTIPLIERS

The bulk of the slot machines in most casinos are coin multipliers, where the potential payouts are multiplied by the number of coins bet. This holds true for all pays except the top jackpot, which is higher than the multiple when the maximum number of coins is played. The purpose, of course, is to encourage the player to bet the maximum on every spin.

For instance, on a three-coin machine, if the top jackpot pays 1000 coins for a one-coin bet, the second coin will pay 2000 coins, but the third coin may pay 4000 coins (instead of 3000 coins), or even 5000 coins or higher. Hence, the usual advice is to always bet the maximum number of coins.

We disagree with that advice when it is given as a blanket rule. You may actually be money ahead by betting only one coin when you play certain machines, such as one with a relatively-low top jackpot. This is true even if you do eventually win that jackpot, which is a remote possibility.

Betting a single coin on a three-coin machine cuts your monetary risk to one-third of what it would have been with a maximum bet. Such an approach may also allow you to move to a higher denomination, and higher denomination machines are usually a little looser.

Thus, by applying some judgement in selecting your machine, you could get a better overall return by betting only one coin.

WILD MULTIPLIER SYMBOLS

As you are examining the payout schedules, searching for that perfect machine, you might enjoy playing one that pays double or triple for certain payline combinations. Such machines have a doubling or tripling substitute (wild) symbol which will multiply the payout for any winning combination. Two doubling symbols on the same payline will quadruple the payout, and two tripling symbols on the same payline will multiply the payout by nine!

In addition to multiplying the payout, these symbols act as wild cards in that they automatically become any other symbol to create a winning combination. Most of these are IGT machines and the most popular ones are called Double Diamond, Triple Diamond, and Red, White & Blue 7s.

Lately, machines with 5x and 10x multipliers are becoming more prevalent. These multipliers operate on the same principle as doubling symbols. For example, if two 10x symbols appear on the same payline, the amount of the payout is multiplied by 100!

Don't confuse the true wild multipliers with machines that have non-multiplying wild symbols such as jokers or wild cherries. Such machines are fine; they just don't provide the excitement of a multiplied jackpot.

OPTION-BUY GAMES

These games are also called Buy-Your-Pay, Buy-A-Pay, as well as various disparaging names. When you bet more than one coin, instead of multiplying the payout, these machines give you additional winning symbol combinations. To get all the possible winning combinations, you must play the maximum number of coins. Unless you do so, the overall payback of the machine is seriously compromised.

Some three-coin option-buy games can be misleading because the second coin is a multiplier, and only the third coin buys you additional symbol combinations. Therefore, on any game you are considering, study the paytable carefully because if is an option-buy, you must never bet less than the maximum.

So why would anyone call an option-buy game bad names? Because many people do not read the paytable carefully, and then they get angry when they bet one coin, hit a winning combination of symbols, and get paid absolutely nothing. A multiplier game would have paid something, even if it was a reduced amount.

Most people tend to get upset when they finally hit a winner and then don't even get paid a nickel. Don't let this happen to you. If you decide to play an option-buy game, be sure you always bet the maximum.

FOUR PRINCIPLES OF BEATING THE SLOTS

Doesn't everyone just drop in the coins and spin the reels? Sure they do, but if you want to come out ahead, or just minimize your losses, you need to know a lot more. If you are primarily a video poker player and haven't paid very much

WIN AT SLOTS

Winning is fun, but like any other gambling game, to get an edge at slots, you have to know what you're doing . Here are some insider tips to get you started.

Read on my friend!

attention to the proliferation of new slot machines, please pay attention to the advice in this chapter.

Following are the four principles of beating the slots.

1. PLAY THE SIMPLE MACHINES

Unless you are willing to give up lesser payoffs in order to shoot for the top jackpot, avoid the progressive machines. We will give you some information on progressives in the next section. You should also avoid most of the fancy, themed video machines. Later on we recommend a few specific machines, but there is such a large variety on the casino floors, that to give you the full story would take an entire book.

The novice slot player should stick to basic three-reel *flat-pay* slots, which are machines that have a fixed top jackpot. To stretch your bankroll, look for two-coin machines with a single payline. As with video poker, playing the maximum number of coins gets you a better return. That is, you have to bet the maximum to qualify for the top jackpot, and sometimes other winning combinations, as well.

If you wish, you can bet the maximum on a three-coin or five-coin machine, but a two-coin slot gives you more spins for your money and more chances of hitting a jackpot. However, keep in mind what we told you about the advantages of playing single coins in the section on coin multipliers, above.

2. SELECTING A SUITABLE MACHINE

Once you have located a row of two-coin, single payline machines in your desired denomination, you should carefully examine the posted payout schedules (known as the *glass*) before you actually start to play. You may be surprised to note how different the payouts are from machine to machine, especially how much the top jackpot changes.

Two side-by-side machines that appear to be basically identical (two-coin, one payline) may have top jackpots of 3000 coins and 8000 coins, respectively. To the inexperienced player, it might seem better to play the one with the highest jackpot. Actually, to compensate for a smaller jackpot, the first machine will have a larger number of small and medium payouts. The two machines may, in fact, have identical overall paybacks.

So which machine should you play?

If you select one with a large jackpot, you can't worry too much about small wins, because you are going for the big one. Just try not to be too disappointed when you don't hit it, because that top jackpot is about as elusive as a royal flush in video poker. If you select a machine with a smaller top jackpot, your bankroll will last longer and fluctuate less because it will be regularly replenished with small and medium wins. We think you will be more satisfied with such a machine.

Finally, before you start to play, check the glass to be sure you didn't inadvertently choose an option-buy game, as described above. This type of machine is not always obvious, especially those versions where the option-buy function only applies to the last coin.

3. FIND THE LOOSEST SLOTS

Unlike video poker machines, you can't look at the payout schedule on a slot machine and tell if it is loose or tight. And when a casino advertises that its slots pay back up to 97% or that some of its slots have a "certified" 98% payback, it's difficult to tell which of the hundreds of machines on the floor are the advertised ones. Actually, you can get in the neighborhood, but it's not nearly as precise as finding the best video poker machines. The secret is (as they say in the real estate business): location, location, location.

In every casino, the slots manager gives considerable thought to the placement of the slot machines. Therefore, to determine where the few loose slots are located on the casino floor, you have to think like the manager. An even better way is to get inside information directly from those slots managers—which is what we have done for you.

Years ago, it was generally known that the best slots were usually located in high-traffic areas—next to the main aisles or near the front entrance—where the greatest number of people would notice the flashing lights and ringing bells of a jackpot winner. Many old-time slots players remember that advice and still seek out machines in those locations. Times have changed, however.

Today, most slot managers place their loosest machines where the greatest number of *slot players* will see and hear them when they pay off. The idea is to motivate the serious slot players so they will keep feeding their machines in the hope that the next big jackpot will be theirs. Consequently, they locate the loose slots next to change booths, on elevated carousels, and anyplace in the center of the slot area where plenty of slots players will notice them when they pay off. Whenever loose slots are in a row, they are usually placed within the first three machines from either end, and never in the middle.

However, not all machines in these locations will be loose, since there are always far fewer loose slots than tight ones. In fact, a typical ratio is 5 to 10 percent loose, 30 to 40 percent tight, with the remainder being mid-range. The best you can do is find the general area where most of the loose machines are likely to be.

Sometimes the managers also put a few loose slots near cafes and coffee shops to encourage players not to dally over their coffee, but to get back to their machines. Keep in mind, however, that a loose slot is always flanked by tight slots, even though the machines appear to be identical. This is done to thwart those people who like to play two side-by-side machines simultaneously.

It is almost as important to know where the tight machines are likely to be placed by the slot manager, so you can avoid them. Anywhere people stand in lines waiting to get into buffets or shows, are prime locations for tight machines. Those people will kill time by idly dropping coins into the machines without really expecting to win—and they won't.

Since many table-game players are distracted and annoyed by the constant clatter of coins, the areas surrounding the table games (especially baccarat and roulette) are populated with tight machines. The same is true of areas near the sportsbook. In fact, any location where the noise of slot machines would disturb non-slot players is apt to have predominately tight machines.

Finally, you must assume that all slot machines located outside of casinos, such as in convenience stores, grocery stores, airports, bars, and restaurants, are very tight. In fact, they are probably the tightest machines in town.

4. TESTING YOUR MACHINE

Once you have found a suitable basic flat-pay machine, it is prudent to first run a simple test to judge whether it is hot or cold. Do this by playing through one roll of 40 quarters ($10) allowing the winnings to collect in the tray, or accumulate as credits. In a two-coin machine, this will amount to 20 spins. In a three-coin machine, you will get 13 spins, with an odd coin left over.

When the roll is finished, count the number of coins that have collected in the tray, or look at how many credits you have accumulated. If your winnings are at least 70% ($7) of what you invested, stick with the machine. If not, move to another machine and repeat the test. Of course, in a dollar machine, your investment will be four times as large, but the testing principle remains the same.

In any case, if after the first five spins of the test you have won nothing, the machine is cold and you should vacate it without carrying the test any further.

If your test winnings are at least 70%, but less than 90%, the machine is marginal and you may want to repeat the test to find out if it's in an *up cycle* or *down cycle*. Should the second test turn out better than the first, the machine is probably in an up cycle. This means the machine is getting hotter, and you should stick with it. Otherwise, abandon the machine. This test does not determine how loose or tight a machine is, but only if it appears to be hot or cold. Even tight machines have hot cycles.

Keep in mind that a hot cycle has a limited life, even on a loose machine. Consequently, you should be prepared to quit a hot machine as soon as it appears to be turning cold. An important clue is that it hasn't paid off in five consecutive spins. In fact, the most conservative players will abandon their machine after four cold spins.

This testing procedure only applies to basic flat-pay machines, and not to progressives. The strategy with progressive slot machines is to go for the main jackpot, with little concern for smaller wins, as explained in the next chapter.

PROGRESSIVE, BONUS & VIDEO SLOTS

PROGRESSIVE SLOTS

In progressive slot machines the top jackpot is not fixed. Progressives are usually part of a linked group of machines, and as the individual slots are played, the jackpot continually grows until

OVERVIEW

There are many types of slot machines available to play. In this chapter, we'll look at the progressive, bonus, and video slots.

We'll start with the progressives.

someone wins it. After a win, the jackpot is reset to a base value and then begins to grow again. Some players are unaware that there is often a secondary jackpot, which is much smaller than the primary.

Progressive slots are typically 2-, 3-, or 5-coin machines, although some nickel machines will take as many as 45 coins. In every case, the maximum number of coins must be bet to qualify for the top prize. Since progressives require a larger bankroll than basic flat pays, we don't recommend them for beginning slots players. The looseness or tightness of a progressive machine is entirely dependent on the current amount of the jackpot, since that determines the overall payback.

Finding the best progressive slot to play is a matter of finding a linked group with the highest jackpot for that type of machine. This is not difficult, since the amount of the top jackpot is prominently displayed on a large digital sign above each bank of progressives, the number continually ticking upward as the players insert coins. A secondary jackpot is shown on a smaller meter, usually below the top jackpot sign.

Each time the jackpot is won, the amount on the meter is reset to a base value. Whenever a jackpot meter (primary or secondary) is close to the base amount, it means there was a recent win and the next win is not likely to occur for some time. You should always try to find a group of machines where the meter shows the greatest dollar increment over the reset value.

The vast majority of progressive players are primarily interested in winning the top jackpot, which can be a lifestyle-changing amount of money. These players consider the smaller wins to be only useful for replenishing their bankrolls so they can stay at their machines for a longer period of time.

Progressive slots, therefore, are not recommended as a brief respite from playing video poker. They have to be approached with a totally different attitude; that is, you can't mind blowing your entire bankroll on the infinitesimal chance of hitting a gigantic payday. It's something like playing the state lottery on a continuous basis.

For those readers who are interested, however, we will provide some basic information on the most popular progressives.

1. Megabucks

These Wide Area Progressive Slots (WAPS) may be found in casinos within each of the major gambling jurisdictions such as Nevada and Mississippi. All the machines in a given jurisdiction are linked to the same huge jackpot pool. Because Megabucks is a three-coin machine, you have to invest $3 on each spin to qualify for the primary jackpot. Line up the four Megabucks symbols on the payline and you win a multi-million dollar jackpot that is paid out in annual installments. After a win, the primary jackpot is reset to $7 million, and the secondary jackpot is reset to $2000.

2. Quartermania

As the name implies, this WAPS accepts quarters, although it takes two of them to qualify for the big payoff, which is paid in twenty annual installments. In Nevada alone, there are more than one thousand of these machines installed, which means it is pretty popular. The primary reset is $1 million, while the secondary is restarted at a measly $1000.

3. Wheel of Fortune

Wheel of Fortune, which pays its top jackpot in annual installments, has become the most popular progressive slot machine in the country. It comes in four denominations, and it takes the maximum number of coins to win the progressive, as follows:

Quarters: Takes three coins and resets to $200,000.

Halves: Takes three coins and resets to $500,000.

Dollars: Takes two coins and resets to $1 million.

5 dollars: Takes two coins and resets to $1 million.

4. Betty Boop's Big Hit

This is Bally's most popular WAPS. Most of the games are multi-denominational, so to qualify for the progressive jackpot, you can bet five nickels, three quarters, or two dollars.

If you think you can beat the system by betting just five nickels, think again. According to Bally, the machines are programmed so that a player who bets two dollars has an eight times better chance of hitting the top jackpot than the player who risks only 25¢ by betting five nickels. Furthermore, the overall theoretical payback rises as the denomination goes up: 84%, 86%, and 88% for nickels, quarters, and dollars, respectively.

After someone hits the progressive, the machine resets to $100,000, and the winner is immediately paid the entire jackpot (less taxes).

5. Addams Family MegaJackpot

If you hit the right combination, this nickel machine will pay out the entire jackpot instantly, but you won't win it unless you put in 45 coins. The progressive reset is $100,000.

BONUS AND VIDEO SLOT MACHINES

The newest and glitziest slot machines on the casino floors have video screens with as many as six simulated reels and as many as 40 paylines. On most machines, a bonus mode appears on a secondary screen when you hit certain symbol combinations. This bonus mode is the only real chance you have to recoup your losses and get ahead.

Other machines have a bonus credit banking mode to encourage you to keep playing in an attempt to reach the big bonus payout before your bankroll is totally depleted.

As you play these computerized wonders, keep in mind that when you bet 45 credits, and the machine noisily announces that you won 36 credits, you are still losing money.

There are special techniques for dealing with bonus video machines that are far too complex to cover in this section. What we will do, however, is list several video slots that you might like to try. Read the Help screen first and bet minimum coins, at least until you have built up some credits and get the hang of the machine. The following are all nickel slots with five reels and up to nine paylines. Hit the right combination, and a bonus screen appears with choices that determine how much you've won.

1. Reel 'Em In

Fishing fun. Bonus screen displays five fishermen. You choose one of them and he/she reels in your bonus.

2. Filthy Rich

A dirty pig farm. To get your bonus, you select one of five dirty pigs and a farmer hoses it down to reveal the amount.

3. Monopoly

Party Train or Once Around versions — Just like the board game. In bonus mode, you work your way around the board, buying properties and collecting bonus points.

4. Chicken

Why does the chicken cross the road? Because you hit the right reel combination to get into the first and second bonus screens, which get you bonuses and free spin credits.

10 ESSENTIAL SLOTS TIPS

1. Be sure to always insert your slot club card.

In some casinos, using your card can effectively increase the payback of the machine you are playing by as much as one percent. You haven't joined the slot club? If you read the section on slot clubs in this book, you will find that there is no down side.

2. Play only what your bankroll can handle.

When you arrive at a gambling resort, you should first ascertain what denomination of machine you should be playing. To help you determine this, the following table shows how much bankroll is needed for a two-, three-, or five-coin bet in each denomination, assuming eight spins per minute and a 90% payout rate:

	2 COINS	3 COINS	5 COINS
5¢ machine	$5/hour	$7/hour	$12/hour
25¢ machine	$24/hour	$36/hour	$60/hour
$1 machine	$96/hour	$144/hour	$240/hour

Next, decide how many hours you would like to play over the course of your stay. For example, assume you start with a bankroll of $1500 and would like to play an average of five hours a day for three days. That is a total of 15 playing hours. Dividing 15 hours into $1500 gives a rate of $100 per hour. Thus, you should not play anything more costly than a two-coin dollar machine. Of course, in actuality, you may win more or lose more than the 90% payback would indicate, but at least you have a reasonable starting point.

3. When you insert coins, be sure you get what you pay for.

Like any equipment with mechanical components, slot machines are subject to considerable wear and tear. This is especially true of the coin mechanism. After handling hundreds of thousands of coins, sooner or later the mechanism will malfunction. Your best protection is to observe the glass and the paylines as you insert each coin to be sure the correct sections light up, showing that they are properly activated.

If you hit a winning combination that doesn't pay because only two of your three coins registered, you are out of luck. If one of your coins doesn't register, be sure to wave down an attendant or press the CHANGE button and wait for someone to arrive. Don't spin the reels before the situation is rectified.

4. Play one machine at a time.

Slot managers know that some people like to play two slots simultaneously, so they always flank a loose machine with tight ones on both sides. At best, you will win from a loose machine only to lose your winnings to a tight one; at worst, you will lose to two tight machines. Two loose machines are never knowingly placed alongside each other.

5. Never play the machine right next to someone who is winning.

If the winner's slot is loose, the machines on either side will be tight. Of course, the winner's machine may just be a moderate payer that turned hot, but you don't know that for certain.

6. Stay with a hot machine.

Never leave a machine that just paid a big jackpot. By definition, it is a hot machine that could continue to pay out very nicely. Follow the rule that we stated in the section on testing: Don't abandon the machine unless it has not paid anything for five consecutive spins.

7. Observe other players who are winning.

Watch players who are winning regularly and keep an eye (and ear) out for sudden jackpot winners. For any number of reasons, these people may occasionally leave *while their machines are still hot*. If you see that happen (and your machine is cold), move over to the other machine before someone else gets there.

Why would a person leave a hot machine? Many slot players think a machine turns cold after paying a big jackpot. Or maybe they have a dinner reservation or tickets for a show. If the machine is still in a hot cycle, their loss is your gain.

8. Abandon a cold machine.

If, after four or five spins, the machine has paid out nothing, abandon it. If available, move over to the slot right next to it. Loose and tight machines are often placed side by side.

9. Never leave a machine that owes you money.

Sometimes when you hit a big jackpot, an attendant has to make the payoff, or sometimes during a payoff, the machine's hopper runs out of coins. *Stay with the machine no matter how long it takes the attendant to arrive.* Occasionally a machine malfunctions and you can't redeem your credits, or the bill acceptor gets hung and eats your Franklin without giving you credits.

Stay with the machine no matter how long it takes for a mechanic to arrive. If you leave the machine, you will have trouble claiming what is rightfully yours.

10. Don't forget to press the CASH OUT button.

Most machines accumulate credits as you play, and you must press the CASH OUT button to convert the credits into coins.

Before leaving the machine, even if you have just won a hand-paid jackpot, be sure to press the CASH OUT button and be sure the credit meter reads zero. If it doesn't, call an attendant because the machine may need a hopper fill, or the coin mechanism may be jammed. If you are distracted when you leave your machine and forget to cash out, someone else will get to enjoy your winnings.

VIDEO POKER PAYOUT SCHEDULES

The following is an item-by-item explanation of every part of the sample payout schedule shown on page 118. The explanations are keyed to the callout letters on the chart and will help you understand how the strategies in this book are presented.

CHAPTER OVERVIEW

This chapter shows the typical payout schedules you will find at the various type of video poker machines. But first, we'll explain how to read the charts.

PAYOUT SCHEDULE EXPLAINED

A — PR-01

This is the designation of the individual chart. The "PR" stands for progressive, and the "01" means that it is the first chart in the Progressive Section of this chapter. In the Jacks-or-Better section, for example, the charts are designated JB-01, JB-02, etc.

B — Strategy PRA

This is the strategy code for the particular machine that this chart represents. "PRA" is the code for a particular strategy table in Chapter 8. The procedure is to first locate the payout schedule that matches your game, note the three-letter strategy code, and then find the correct strategy table in Chapter 8.

Some of the low-paying schedules show a strategy code of "NR" (for *not recommended*) and have no associated strategy chart. These schedules are included for reference purposes—to help you recognize a poor-paying machine when you see it.

C — 1 Coin, 5 Coins

These columns show the payouts (in number of coins) for each winning hand, depending on whether you bet one coin or five coins.

To simplify the charts, only one-coin and five-coin payouts are shown. If you need to know the two, three, or four-coin payouts they are easy to derive: simply multiply the number of coins by the amount in the one-coin column. Keep in mind, however, that the payback percentages shown at the bottom of the chart are for 5-coin play.

D — Progressive Sequential Royal

Sequential means that the cards that make up a royal flush have to appear on the video screen in sequential order, such as 10-J-Q-K-A or A-K-Q-J-10. Whether the sequence has to be ten-to-ace or ace-to-ten is defined on the particular machine.

Progressive means that the payout for this winning hand is the amount shown on the progressive meter (in dollars) above the bank of machines. Note that this sample schedule has two different progressive payouts, depending on whether the royal flush is suited or unsuited (see below).

E — Suited

The term *suited* means that all the cards in the royal flush have to be of a pre-defined suit, rather than any of the four suits. The machine defines which suit is required for the hand to be a winner. For instance, if the display or posted schedule states that a suited royal has to be hearts, then a royal in spades, diamonds, or clubs is not a suited winner, but instead, would be an unsuited winner. In some schedules, the suited requirement may also be applied to straight flushes.

F — Unsuited

The term *unsuited* means that the royal flush can be any of the four suits, as long as all the cards that make up the royal are of the same suit.

G — Jackpot Reset

This is the starting point of the progressive meter. It is the value to which the meter is reset immediately after the progressive jackpot has been won.

H — 100% Payback

When the progressive meter reaches the value shown, the overall payback of the machine is theoretically 100%. As the progressive meter climbs above this value, the machine payback exceeds 100%. If you find a progressive meter at this level, it will also be difficult to find an open machine.

I — Royal Flush

This is the standard royal flush that is also found on non-progressive machines. It is neither sequential nor suited. The five cards that make up the royal (10-J-Q-K-A) must all be of the same suit, but may appear on the video screen in any order.

J — Payback: 95.8% at reset

This is the overall payback of the machine when the progressive meter is at it's lowest value, which is the jackpot reset amount defined above. This calculated payback percentage is based on long-term play using perfect strategy and betting the maximum number of coins (usually five). For short-term adjustments, see the Short Term Payback Correction tables.

K — 95.5% w/o Sequential Royals

This is the overall payback of the machine without including the effect of the sequential royal flushes, which are very rare hands. It is a more realistic number for the average player who never wins a sequential progressive. This number does not change as the progressive meter climbs in value.

L — Note: Progressive Payouts

Most progressive machines come in quarter and dollar denominations, and sometimes you will see a five-dollar machine. To keep the charts simple, only the progressive payouts for quarter machines are shown. The equivalent payouts for dollar machines are four times as high, and for five-dollar machines are 20 times as high. For the non-progressive winning hands, the payouts do not vary with the bet denomination because they are shown in terms of the number of coins paid out, rather than dollar amounts.

HOW TO USE THE CHARTS IN THIS CHAPTER

This chapter contains charts detailing the payout schedules of the most common video poker games found in the major casinos. The charts are organized by category to help you match the correct chart to a particular game. First look at a video poker machine to determine what kind of game it is (Original Jacks or Better, Bonus Quads, Deuces Wild, etc.) and then flip through this chapter until you find that category. The first page of each section lists typical descriptive names as a double check that you are in the right place.

The individual charts in the larger sections are sorted to make the correct chart easier to locate. For example, in the Bonus Quads section the charts are in order of the highest quad (four-of-a-kind) payout. The ordering of the charts is explained on the introductory page for each section. When you are in the right section, compare the payout schedule posted on the machine to the payout charts shown. Once the correct schedule is found, it will give you the long-term payback percentage and the associated strategy code for that game.

SAMPLE PAYOUT SCHEDULE

POKERMANIA:

D Progressive Sequential Royal (suited) **E**

at jackpot reset: $100,000 **G**

at 100% payback: $800,000. **H**

Progressive Sequential Royal (unsuited) **F**

at jackpot reset: $1000 **G**

at 100% payback: $8000 **H**

PR-01 **A**	Strategy PRA **B**	1 coin	5 coins **C**
I Royal Flush		250	4000
Straight Flush		100	500
Quad Aces		160	800
Quad 2, 3, or 4		80	400
Quad 5 thru King		50	250
Full House		8	40
Flush		6	30
Straight		4	20
Three of a Kind		3	15
Two Pairs		1	5
Jacks or Better		1	5

Payback: 95.8% at reset **J**

95.5% w/o sequential royals. **K**

L Note: Progressive payouts are for quarter machines. For dollars, multiply by four.

MAJOR CATEGORIES:
Original Jacks Or Better
Tens Or Better
Two Pairs Or Better
Bonus Quads
Bonus Royals
Deuces Wild
Joker Wild
Deuces And Joker Wild
Double Joker
Five Deck Poker
Progressive Jackpot

NOTES

Strategy tables are located in the Playing Strategy Tables chapter.

Strategy NR means no strategy is provided because this version is not recommended. Schedule is shown for reference only.

Payback percentages are for perfect strategy and 5-coin play.

Payback percentages are based on long-term play. For short-term adjustments, see the short-term payback correction tables.

ORIGINAL JACKS OR BETTER

This was the initial form of video poker and is still very popular today. The lowest paying hand is a pair of jacks, and there are no wild cards. The payout schedules are based on standard poker hands. Most of these machines come in a variety of paybacks from good (97-98%) to excellent (99-100%).

Note: The charts in this section are grouped by the payout for Full House, Flush, and Two Pairs. These payouts are shown in **bold** type.

TYPICAL DESCRIPTIVE NAMES:

- All American Poker
- Bonus Poker Deluxe
- Bonus Triple Play
- Draw Poker
- Jacks Or Better
- Players Choice
- Players Edge Draw Poker

ORIGINAL JACKS OR BETTER

JB-01	Strategy **JBA**	1 coin	5 coins
Royal Flush		250	***
Straight Flush		50	250
Four-of-a-Kind		25	125
Full House		**9**	**45**
Flush		**6**	**30**
Straight		4	20
Three of a Kind		3	15
Two Pairs		**2**	**10**
Jacks or Better		1	5

*** Payback: 99.5% for 4000
99.8% for 4700

JB-02	Strategy **JBA**	1 coin	5 coins
Royal Flush		250	***
Straight Flush		50	250
Four-of-a-Kind		25	125
Full House		**9**	**45**
Flush		**5**	**25**
Straight		4	20
Three of a Kind		3	15
Two Pairs		**2**	**10**
Jacks or Better		1	5

*** Payback: 98.5% for 4000
98.8% for 4700

ORIGINAL JACKS OR BETTER

JB-03	Strategy **JBA**	1 coin	5 coins
Royal Flush		250	***
Straight Flush		50	250
Four-of-a-Kind		25	125
Full House		**8**	**40**
Flush		**5**	**25**
Straight		4	20
Three of a Kind		3	15
Two Pairs		**2**	**10**
Jacks or Better		1	5

*** Payback: 97.3% for 4000
97.6% for 4700
97.8% for 5000

JB-04	Strategy **JBA**	1 coin	5 coins
Royal Flush		250	***
Straight Flush		50	250
Four-of-a-Kind		25	125
Full House		**6**	**30**
Flush		**5**	**25**
Straight		4	20
Three of a Kind		3	15
Two Pairs		**2**	**10**
Jacks or Better		1	5

*** Payback: 95.0% for 4000
95.3% for 4700
95.5% for 5000

ORIGINAL JACKS OR BETTER

JB-05	Strategy JBA	1 coin	5 coins
Royal Flush		250	***
Straight Flush		50	250
Four-of-a-Kind		80	400
Full House		**8**	**40**
Flush		**6**	**30**
Straight		4	20
Three of a Kind		3	15
Two Pairs		**1**	**5**
Jacks or Better		1	5

*** Payback: 98.5% for 4000
98.8% for 4700

JB-06	Strategy JBA	1 coin	5 coins
Royal Flush		250	***
Straight Flush		50	250
Four-of-a-Kind		80	400
Full House		**8**	**40**
Flush		**5**	**25**
Straight		4	20
Three of a Kind		3	15
Two Pairs		**1**	**5**
Jacks or Better		1	5

*** Payback: 97.4% for 4000
97.7% for 4700

ORIGINAL JACKS OR BETTER

JB-07	Strategy **JBA**	1 coin	5 coins
Royal Flush		250	***
Straight Flush		50	250
Four-of-a-Kind		80	400
Full House		**7**	**35**
Flush		**5**	**25**
Straight		4	20
Three of a Kind		3	15
Two Pairs		**1**	**5**
Jacks or Better		1	5

*** Payback: 96.3% for 4000
96.6% for 4700
96.8% for 5000

JB-08	Strategy **NR**	1 coin	5 coins
Royal Flush		250	***
Straight Flush		50	250
Four-of-a-Kind		25	125
Full House		**8**	**40**
Flush		**5**	**25**
Straight		4	20
Three of a Kind		3	15
Two Pairs		**1**	**5**
Jacks or Better		1	5

*** Payback: 84.4% for 4000
84.7% for 4700
84.9% for 5000

ORIGINAL JACKS OR BETTER

JB-09	Strategy **JBB**	1 coin	5 coins
Royal Flush		250	***
Straight Flush		200	1000
Four-of-a-Kind		40	200
Full House		**8**	**40**
Flush		**8**	**40**
Straight		8	40
Three of a Kind		3	15
Two Pairs		**1**	**5**
Jacks or Better		1	5

*** Payback: 100.7% for 4000
101.1% for 4700

JB-10	Strategy **JBB**	1 coin	5 coins
Royal Flush		250	***
Straight Flush		200	1000
Four-of-a-Kind		30	150
Full House		**8**	**40**
Flush		**8**	**40**
Straight		8	40
Three of a Kind		3	15
Two Pairs		**1**	**5**
Jacks or Better		1	5

*** Payback: 98.5% for 4000
98.8% for 4700

ORIGINAL JACKS OR BETTER

JB-11	Strategy NR	1 coin	5 coins
Royal Flush		500	2500
Straight Flush		100	500
Four-of-a-Kind		35	175
Full House		**10**	**50**
Flush		**7**	**35**
Straight		6	30
Three of a Kind		3	15
Two Pairs		**1**	**5**
Jacks or Better		1	5

Payback: 94.6%

JB-12	Strategy NR	1 coin	5 coins
Royal Flush		500	2500
Straight Flush		100	500
Four-of-a-Kind		25	125
Full House		**10**	**50**
Flush		**8**	**40**
Straight		6	30
Three of a Kind		3	15
Two Pairs		**1**	**5**
Jacks or Better		1	5

Payback: 94.0%
In Louisiana, where max jackpot is $500, don't
play more than 4 quarters or 1 dollar.

TENS OR BETTER

This is basically the same as jacks or better except that the lowest paying hand is a pair of tens. Some (but not all) tens-or-better machines have excellent paybacks (99%), if you can find one of them.

> **TYPICAL DESCRIPTIVE NAMES:**
> • Draw Poker
> • Tens Or Better

TENS OR BETTER

TB-01	Strategy **TBA**	1 coin	5 coins
Royal Flush		250	***
Straight Flush		50	250
Four-of-a-Kind		25	125
Full House		6	30
Flush		5	25
Straight		4	20
Three of a Kind		3	15
Two Pairs		2	10
Tens or Better		1	5

*** Payback: 99.1% for 4000
99.4% for 4700

TB-02	Strategy **TBA**	1 coin	5 coins
Royal Flush		250	***
Straight Flush		50	250
Four-of-a-Kind		25	125
Full House		9	45
Flush		6	30
Straight		4	20
Three of a Kind		3	15
Two Pairs		1	5
Tens or Better		1	5

*** Payback: 90.8% for 4000
91.1% for 4700

TWO PAIRS OR BETTER

The name tells the tale. The lowest paying hand is two pairs. The best of these machines has a pretty good payback of 98%, but there are also poorer versions. You will often find two-pairs scattered among the jacks-or-better machines, since some players don't seem to know the difference.

TYPICAL DESCRIPTIVE NAMES:
 • Draw Poker

TWO PAIRS OR BETTER

TP-01	Strategy **TPA**	1 coin	5 coins
Royal Flush		250	***
Straight Flush		100	500
Four-of-a-Kind		50	250
Full House		12	60
Flush		8	40
Straight		6	30
Three of a Kind		3	15
Two Pairs		2	10

*** Payback: 98.1% for 4000
98.4% for 4700

TP-02	Strategy **TPA**	1 coin	5 coins
Royal Flush		250	***
Straight Flush		100	500
Four-of-a-Kind		50	250
Full House		11	55
Flush		7	35
Straight		5	25
Three of a Kind		3	15
Two Pairs		2	10

*** Payback: 93.5% for 4000
93.7% for 4700

BONUS QUADS

Bonus Quads are jacks-or-better machines that offer extra-high payouts for specific four-of-a-kind (quad) hands. With most versions in Nevada paying back 98-100%, Bonus Quads have become very popular. Most versions found in Atlantic City and along the Mississippi, however, typically pay about 94 to 98%.

Note: The charts in this section are in order of the top quad payout (in **bold** type), from the lowest to the highest.

> **TYPICAL DESCRIPTIVE NAMES:**
> · Aces And Eights
> · Aces And Faces
> · Aces And Jacks
> · Aces Bonus Poker
> · Bonus Deuces
> · Bonus Poker
> · Double Bonus Poker
> · Double Bonus Plus
> · Double Bonus Jackpot
> · Double Double Bonus Poker
> · Double Double Jackpot
> · Flush Attack
> · Fours Plus
> · Nevada Bonus Poker
> · Power House Poker
> · Triple Bonus Poker
> · Triple Poker
> · Super Aces
> · White Hot Aces

BONUS QUADS

BQ-01	Strategy **BQA**	1 coin	5 coins
Royal Flush		250	4000
Straight Flush		100	500
Quad Aces		**50**	**250**
Quad 2, 3, or 4		40	200
Quad 5 thru King		20	100
Full House		8	40
Flush		5	25
Straight		4	20
Three of a Kind		3	15
Two Pairs		2	10
Jacks or Better		1	5

Payback: 98.3%

BQ-02	Strategy **BQB**	1 coin	5 coins
Royal Flush		250	4000
Straight Flush		50	250
Quad Deuces		**50**	**250**
Quad 3, 4, or 5		40	200
Quad 6 thru Ace		25	125
Full House		6	40
Flush		5	25
Straight		4	20
Three of a Kind		3	15
Two Pairs		2	10
Jacks or Better		1	5

Payback: 96.2%

BONUS QUADS

BQ-03	Strategy **BQC**	1 coin	5 coins
Royal Flush		250	4000
Straight Flush		50	250
Quad Aces		**80**	**400**
Quad Kings		60	300
Quad Queens		40	200
Quad 2 thru Jack		20	100
Full House		8	40
Flush		6	30
Straight		4	20
Three of a Kind		3	15
Two Pairs		2	10
Jacks or Better		1	5
Payback: 99.6%			

BQ-04	Strategy **BQC**	1 coin	5 coins
Royal Flush		250	4000
Straight Flush		50	250
Quad Aces		**80**	**400**
Quad K, Q, or Jack		40	200
Quad 2 thru 10		25	125
Full House		8	40
Flush		5	25
Straight		4	20
Three of a Kind		3	15
Two Pairs		2	10
Jacks or Better		1	5
Payback: 99.3%			

BONUS QUADS

BQ-05	Strategy **BQC**	1 coin	5 coins
Royal Flush		250	4000
Straight Flush		50	250
Quad Aces		**80**	**400**
Quad 2, 3, or 4		40	200
Quad 5 thru King		25	125
Full House		8	40
Flush		5	25
Straight		4	20
Three of a Kind		3	15
Two Pairs		2	10
Jacks or Better		1	5

Payback: 99.2%

BQ-06	Strategy **BQB**	1 coin	5 coins
Royal Flush		250	4000
Straight Flush		50	250
Quad Deuces		**80**	**400**
Quad 3, 4, or 5		40	200
Quad 6 thru Ace		25	125
Full House		7	35
Flush		5	25
Straight		4	20
Three of a Kind		3	15
Two Pairs		2	10
Jacks or Better		1	5

Payback: 97.9%

BONUS QUADS

BQ-07	Strategy **BQC**	1 coin	5 coins
Royal Flush		250	4000
Straight Flush		50	250
Quad Aces		**80**	**400**
Quad 2, 3, or 4		40	200
Quad 5 thru King		25	125
Full House		6	30
Flush		5	25
Straight		4	20
Three of a Kind		3	15
Two Pairs		2	10
Jacks or Better		1	5
Payback: 96.9%			

BQ-08	Strategy **BQB**	1 coin	5 coins
Royal Flush		250	4000
Straight Flush		50	250
Quad Deuces		**80**	**400**
Quad 3, 4, or 5		40	200
Quad 6 thru Ace		25	125
Full House		6	30
Flush		5	25
Straight		4	20
Three of a Kind		3	15
Two Pairs		2	10
Jacks or Better		1	5
Payback: 96.8%			

BONUS QUADS

BQ-09	Strategy **BQC**	1 coin	5 coins
Royal Flush		250	4000
Straight Flush		50	250
Quad Aces		**100**	**500**
Quad Jacks		50	250
Quad 2 thru 10, Q, K		25	125
Full House		8	40
Flush		5	25
Straight		4	20
Three of a Kind		3	15
Two Pairs		2	10
Jacks or Better		1	5

Payback: 99.3%

BQ-10	Strategy **BQD**	1 coin	5 coins
Royal Flush		250	4000
Straight Flush		50	250
Quad Aces		**160**	**800**
Quad 2, 3, or 4		80	400
Quad 5 thru King		50	250
Full House		8	40
Flush (with light on)		25	125
Flush (with light off)		5	25
Straight		4	20
Three of a Kind		3	15
Two Pairs		1	5
Jacks or Better		1	5

Payback: 134% when FLUSH light is ON.
94.2% when light is OFF.

BONUS QUADS

BQ-11	Strategy **BQE**	1 coin	5 coins
Royal Flush		250	4000
Straight Flush		50	250
Quad Aces		**160**	**800**
Quad 2, 3, or 4		80	400
Quad 5 thru King		50	250
Full House		10	50
Flush		7	35
Straight		5	25
Three of a Kind		3	15
Two Pairs		1	5
Jacks or Better		1	5

Payback: 100.1%

BQ-12	Strategy **BQE**	1 coin	5 coins
Royal Flush		250	4000
Straight Flush		50	250
Quad Aces		**160**	**800**
Quad 2, 3, or 4		80	400
Quad 5 thru King		50	250
Full House		8	40
Flush		5	25
Straight		4	20
Three of a Kind		2	10
Two Pairs		2	10
Jacks or Better		1	5

Payback: 99.5%

BONUS QUADS

BQ-13	Strategy BQC	1 coin	5 coins
Royal Flush		250	4000
Straight Flush		50	250
Quad Aces w/ J,Q,or K		**160**	**640**
Quad Aces		80	400
Quad K,Q,or J w/J,Q,K,or A		80	400
Quad K,Q,or J		40	200
Quad 2 thru 10		20	100
Full House		8	40
Flush		5	25
Straight		4	20
Three of a Kind		3	15
Two Pairs		2	10
Jacks or Better		1	5

Payback: 99.4%

BQ-14	Strategy BQE	1 coin	5 coins
Royal Flush		250	4000
Straight Flush		50	250
Quad Aces		**160**	**800**
Quad 2, 3, or 4		80	400
Quad 5 thru King		50	250
Full House		9	45
Flush		7	35
Straight		5	25
Three of a Kind		3	15
Two Pairs		1	5
Jacks or Better		1	5

Payback: 99.1%

BONUS QUADS

BQ-15	Strategy **BQE**	1 coin	5 coins
Royal Flush		250	4000
Straight Flush		50	250
Quad Aces		**160**	**800**
Quad 2, 3, or 4		80	400
Quad 5 thru King		50	250
Full House		9	45
Flush		6	30
Straight		5	25
Three of a Kind		3	15
Two Pairs		1	5
Jacks or Better		1	5

Payback: 97.8%

BQ-16	Strategy **BQE**	1 coin	5 coins
Royal Flush		250	4000
Straight Flush		50	250
Quad Aces		**160**	**800**
Quad 2, 3, or 4		80	400
Quad 5 thru King		50	250
Full House		8	40
Flush		6	30
Straight		5	25
Three of a Kind		3	15
Two Pairs		1	5
Jacks or Better		1	5

Payback: 96.7%

BONUS QUADS

BQ-17	Strategy **BQE**	1 coin	5 coins
Royal Flush		250	4000
Straight Flush		50	250
Quad Aces		**160**	**800**
Quad 2, 3, or 4		80	400
Quad 5 thru King		50	250
Full House		9	45
Flush		6	30
Straight		4	20
Three of a Kind		3	15
Two Pairs		1	5
Jacks or Better		1	5

Payback: 96.4%

BQ-18	Strategy **BQF**	1 coin	5 coins
Royal Flush		250	4000
Straight Flush		50	250
Quad Aces		**240**	**1200**
Quad 2, 3, or 4		120	600
Quad 5 thru King		75	375
Full House		11	55
Flush		7	35
Straight		4	20
Three of a Kind		3	15
Two Pairs		1	5
Kings or Better		1	5

Payback: 99.6%
Note lowest hand is Kings or Better.

BONUS QUADS

BQ-19	Strategy **BQF**	1 coin	5 coins
Royal Flush		250	4000
Straight Flush		50	250
Quad Aces		**240**	**1200**
Quad 2, 3, or 4		120	600
Quad 5 thru King		75	375
Full House		10	50
Flush		7	35
Straight		4	20
Three of a Kind		3	15
Two Pairs		1	5
Kings or Better		1	5

Payback: 98.5%
Note lowest hand is Kings or Better.

BQ-20	Strategy **BQG**	1 coin	5 coins
Royal Flush		250	4000
Straight Flush		80	400
Quad Aces		**240**	**1200**
Quad 2, 3, or 4		120	600
Quad 5 thru King		50	250
Full House		8	40
Flush		5	25
Straight		4	20
Three of a Kind		3	15
Two Pairs		1	5
Jacks or Better		1	5

Payback: 98.5%

BONUS QUADS

BQ-21	Strategy **BQG**	1 coin	5 coins
Royal Flush		250	4000
Straight Flush		50	250
Quad Aces		**240**	**1200**
Quad 2, 3, or 4		120	600
Quad 5 thru King		50	250
Full House		8	40
Flush		5	25
Straight		4	20
Three of a Kind		3	15
Two Pairs		1	5
Jacks or Better		1	5

Payback: 98.2%

BQ-22	Strategy **BQG**	1 coin	5 coins
Royal Flush		250	4000
Straight Flush		50	250
Quad Aces		**240**	**1200**
Quad 2, 3, or 4		120	600
Quad 5 thru King		50	250
Full House		6	30
Flush		5	25
Straight		4	20
Three of a Kind		3	15
Two Pairs		1	5
Jacks or Better		1	5

Payback: 96.1%

BONUS QUADS

BQ-23	Strategy **BQG**	1 coin	5 coins
Royal Flush		250	4000
Straight Flush		50	250
Quad Aces		**400**	**2000**
Quad 2, 3, or 4		80	400
Quad 5 thru King		50	250
Full House		8	40
Flush		5	25
Straight		4	20
Three of a Kind		3	15
Two Pairs		1	5
Jacks or Better		1	5

Payback: 99.8%

BQ-24	Strategy **BQH**	1 coin	5 coins
Royal Flush		250	4000
Straight Flush		50	250
Quad Aces w/ 2,3,or 4		**400**	**2000**
Quad Aces		160	800
Quad 2,3,or 4 w/A,2,3,or 4		160	800
Quad 2,3,or 4		80	400
Quad 5 thru King		50	250
Full House		9	45
Flush		6	30
Straight		4	20
Three of a Kind		3	15
Two Pairs		1	5
Jacks or Better		1	5

Payback: 98.8%

BONUS QUADS

BQ-25	Strategy **BQH**	1 coin	5 coins
Royal Flush		250	4000
Straight Flush		50	250
Quad Aces w/ 2,3,or 4		**400**	**2000**
Quad Aces		160	800
Quad 2,3,or 4 w/A,2,3,or 4		160	800
Quad 2,3,or 4		80	400
Quad 5 thru K		50	250
Full House		9	45
Flush		5	25
Straight		4	20
Three of a Kind		3	15
Two Pairs		1	5
Jacks or Better		1	5
Payback: 97.7%			

BQ-26	Strategy **BQH**	1 coin	5 coins
Royal Flush		250	4000
Straight Flush		50	250
Quad Aces w/ 2,3,or 4		**400**	**2000**
Quad Aces		160	800
Quad 2,3,or 4 w/A,2,3,or 4		160	800
Quad 2,3,or 4		80	400
Quad 5 thru K		50	250
Full House		8	40
Flush		5	25
Straight		4	20
Three of a Kind		3	15
Two Pairs		1	5
Jacks or Better		1	5
Payback: 96.6%			

BONUS ROYALS

This is a small category of bonus machines that have extra-high payouts for specified royal flushes. Most pay back in the range of 99 to 100 percent, but depend on combinations that occur less often, such as a sequential royal flush. The games in this category are non-progressive. The Progressive Jackpot category contains similar games, which are designed to build the jackpot value very high before someone wins it.

TYPICAL DESCRIPTIVE NAMES:
- Bonus Flush
- Bonus Pay Bonanza
- Double Pay Diamonds HI
- Hi-low RoyalR
- Reversible RoyalW
- Wrap A Royal

BONUS ROYALS

BR-01	Strategy **BRA**	1 coin	5 coins
Royal Flush (suited)		500	10000
Royal Flush		250	5000
Straight Flush (suited)		100	500
Straight Flush		50	250
Four of a Kind		25	125
Full House		8	40
Flush (suited)		10	50
Flush		5	25
Straight		4	20
Three of a Kind		3	15
Two Pairs		2	10
Jacks or Better		1	5

Payback: 99.7%

BR-02	Strategy **BRB**	1 coin	5 coins
Royal Flush (wrapped)		500	8000
Royal Flush		250	4000
Straight Flush		50	250
Quad Aces (grouped)		320	1600
Quad Aces		160	800
Quad w/ 2, 3, or 4		80	400
Quad w/ 5 thru King		50	250
Full House		9	45
Flush		6	30
Straight		5	25
Three of a Kind		3	15
Two Pairs		1	5
Jacks or Better		1	5

Payback: 99.4% (Note: Wrapped RF is a reversible sequential starting at any card.)

BONUS ROYALS

BR-03	Strategy **BRC**	1 coin	5 coins
Royal Flush		250	4000
Low Royal (2 thru 6)		250	4000
Straight Flush		50	250
Four of a Kind		40	200
Full House		6	30
Flush		5	25
Straight		4	20
Three of a Kind		3	15
Two Pairs		2	10
Jacks or Better		1	5

Payback: 99.8%

BR-04	Strategy **BRC**	1 coin	5 coins
Royal Flush		250	4000
Low Royal (2 thru 6)		250	4000
Straight Flush		50	250
Four of a Kind		30	150
Full House		6	30
Flush		5	25
Straight		4	20
Three of a Kind		3	15
Two Pairs		2	10
Jacks or Better		1	5

Payback: 97.5%

DEUCES WILD

In this game all four deuces are wild cards. A royal flush with deuces, called a deuce royal, pays much less than a natural. All other hands pay the same with or without deuces. Even though the lowest-paying hand is three-of-a-kind, many versions of deuces wild have an excellent payback of 99 to 101%. But watch out for those that pay only 94 to 96%.

Note: The charts in this section are in order of the four deuces payout (in **bold** type) from the lowest to the highest.

TYPICAL DESCRIPTIVE NAMES:
- Bonus Deuces
- Deuces Deluxe
- Deuces Wild Poker
- Deuces Wild Bonus Poker
- Double Pay Deuces
- Loose Deuces

DEUCES WILD

DW-01	Strategy DWA	1 coin	5 coins
Natural Royal Flush		250	4000
Four Deuces		**200**	**1000**
Deuce Royal Flush		25	125
Five of a Kind		15	75
Straight Flush		9	45
Four of a Kind		5	25
Full House		3	15
Flush		2	10
Straight		2	10
Three of a Kind		1	5

Payback: 100.6%

DW-02	Strategy DWB	1 coin	5 coins
Natural Royal Flush		250	4000
Four Deuces		**200**	**1000**
Deuce Royal Flush		20	100
Five of a Kind		12	60
Straight Flush		9	45
Four of a Kind		5	25
Full House		3	15
Flush		2	10
Straight		2	10
Three of a Kind		1	5

Payback: 98.9%

DEUCES WILD

DW-03	Strategy **DWC**	1 coin	5 coins
Natural Royal Flush		250	4000
Four Deuces		**200**	**1000**
Deuce Royal Flush		25	125
Five of a Kind		16	80
Straight Flush		13	65
Four of a Kind		4	20
Full House		4	20
Flush		3	15
Straight		2	10
Three of a Kind		1	5

Payback: 96.8%

DW-04	Strategy **DWC**	1 coin	5 coins
Natural Royal Flush		250	4000
Four Deuces		**200**	**1000**
Deuce Royal Flush		25	125
Five of a Kind		16	80
Straight Flush		13	65
Four of a Kind		4	20
Full House		3	15
Flush		2	10
Straight		2	10
Three of a Kind		1	5

Payback: 96.8%

DEUCES WILD

DW-05	Strategy **DWD**	1 coin	5 coins
Natural Royal Flush		250	4000
Four Deuces		**200**	**1000**
Deuce Royal Flush		20	100
Five of a Kind		10	50
Straight Flush		8	40
Four of a Kind		4	20
Full House		4	20
Flush		3	15
Straight		2	10
Three of a Kind		1	5

Payback: 96.0%

DW-06	Strategy **NR**	1 coin	5 coins
Natural Royal Flush		250	4000
Four Deuces		**200**	**1000**
Deuce Royal Flush		25	125
Five of a Kind		15	75
Straight Flush		10	50
Four of a Kind		4	20
Full House		3	15
Flush		2	10
Straight		2	10
Three of a Kind		1	5

Payback: 94.8%

DEUCES WILD

DW-07	Strategy **NR**	1 coin	5 coins
Natural Royal Flush		250	4000
Four Deuces		**200**	**1000**
Deuce Royal Flush		25	125
Five of a Kind		15	75
Straight Flush		9	45
Four of a Kind		4	20
Full House		3	15
Flush		2	10
Straight		2	10
Three of a Kind		1	5

Payback: 94.3%

DW-08	Strategy **NR**	1 coin	5 coins
Natural Royal Flush		250	4000
Four Deuces		**200**	**1000**
Deuce Royal Flush		20	100
Five of a Kind		10	50
Straight Flush		8	40
Four of a Kind		4	20
Full House		4	20
Flush		2	10
Straight		2	10
Three of a Kind		1	5

Payback: 94.0%

DEUCES WILD

DW-09	Strategy **DWD**	1 coin	5 coins
Natural Royal Flush		250	4000
Four Deuces		**400**	**2000**
Deuce Royal Flush		20	100
Five of a Kind		10	50
Straight Flush		10	50
Four of a Kind		4	20
Full House		4	20
Flush		3	15
Straight		2	10
Three of a Kind		1	5

Payback: 101.0%

DW-10	Strategy **DWE**	1 coin	5 coins
Natural Royal Flush		250	4000
Four Deuces		**400**	**2000**
Deuce Royal Flush		25	125
Five of a Kind		16	80
Straight Flush		11	55
Four of a Kind		4	20
Full House		3	15
Flush		2	10
Straight		2	10
Three of a Kind		1	5

Payback: 99.6%

DEUCES WILD

DW-11	Strategy **DWE**	1 coin	5 coins
Natural Royal Flush		250	4000
Four Deuces		**500**	**2500**
Deuce Royal Flush		25	125
Five of a Kind		15	75
Straight Flush		10	50
Four of a Kind		4	20
Full House		3	15
Flush		2	10
Straight		2	10
Three of a Kind		1	5

Payback: 101.0%

DW-12	Strategy **DWE**	1 coin	5 coins
Natural Royal Flush		250	4000
Four Deuces		**500**	**2500**
Deuce Royal Flush		25	125
Five of a Kind		12	60
Straight Flush		8	40
Four of a Kind		4	20
Full House		3	15
Flush		2	10
Straight		2	10
Three of a Kind		1	5

Payback: 99.2%

JOKER WILD

This game uses a 53-card deck in which the joker is a wild card. The joker can be substituted for any other card in the deck, except that a royal flush with a joker does not pay as well as a natural. Although some joker machines pay 99-102%, many of them pay in the range of 94 to 97%.

Note: The charts in this section are grouped by the lowest hand: *Two Pairs* or *Kings or Better*.

TYPICAL DESCRIPTIVE NAMES:
- Bonus Quints
- Joker Poker

JOKER WILD - TWO PAIRS

JW-01	Strategy JWA	1 coin	5 coins
Natural Royal Flush		500	***
Five of a Kind		100	500
Joker Royal Flush		50	250
Straight Flush		50	250
Four of a Kind		20	100
Full House		8	40
Flush		7	35
Straight		6	30
Three of a Kind		2	10
Two Pairs		1	5

*** Payback: 101.6% for 4000
101.9% for 4700
102.0% for 5000

JW-02	Strategy JWA	1 coin	5 coins
Natural Royal Flush		500	***
Five of a Kind		100	500
Joker Royal Flush		50	250
Straight Flush		50	250
Four of a Kind		20	100
Full House		10	50
Flush		6	30
Straight		5	25
Three of a Kind		2	10
Two Pairs		1	5

*** Payback: 99.4% for 4000
99.7% for 4700
99.8% for 5000

JOKER WILD - TWO PAIRS

JW-03	Strategy **JWA**	1 coin	5 coins
Natural Royal Flush		500	***
Five of a Kind		100	500
Joker Royal Flush		50	250
Straight Flush		50	250
Four of a Kind		20	100
Full House		8	40
Flush		7	35
Straight		5	25
Three of a Kind		2	10
Two Pairs		1	5

*** Payback: 98.7% for 4000
            98.9% for 4700
            99.1% for 5000

JW-04	Strategy **JWB**	1 coin	5 coins
Five of a Kind		400	***
Natural Royal Flush		100	500
Joker Royal Flush		100	500
Straight Flush		100	500
Four of a Kind		16	80
Full House		8	40
Flush		5	25
Straight		4	20
Three of a Kind		2	10
Two Pairs		1	5

*** Payback: 97.2% for 4000
           98.3% for 4700
           98.9% for 5000

JOKER WILD - TWO PAIRS

JW-05	Strategy **JWA**	1 coin	5 coins
Natural Royal Flush		500	***
Five of a Kind		100	500
Joker Royal Flush		50	250
Straight Flush		50	250
Four of a Kind		20	100
Full House		8	40
Flush		6	30
Straight		5	25
Three of a Kind		2	10
Two Pairs		1	5

*** Payback: 96.4% for 4000
96.7% for 4700
96.8% for 5000

JW-06	Strategy **JWA**	1 coin	5 coins
Natural Royal Flush		500	***
Five of a Kind		100	500
Joker Royal Flush		50	250
Straight Flush		50	250
Four of a Kind		25	125
Full House		8	40
Flush		5	25
Straight		4	20
Three of a Kind		2	10
Two Pairs		1	5

*** Payback: 95.6% for 4000
95.9% for 4700
96.0% for 5000

JOKER WILD - TWO PAIRS

JW-07	Strategy JWA	1 coin	5 coins
Natural Royal Flush		500	***
Five of a Kind		100	500
Joker Royal Flush		50	250
Straight Flush		50	250
Four of a Kind		20	100
Full House		8	40
Flush		6	30
Straight		4	20
Three of a Kind		2	10
Two Pairs		1	5

*** Payback: 93.6% for 4000
93.9% for 4700
94.0% for 5000

JW-08	Strategy JWB	1 coin	5 coins
Five of a Kind		400	***
Natural Royal Flush		100	500
Joker Royal Flush		100	500
Straight Flush		100	500
Four of a Kind		15	75
Full House		6	30
Flush		5	25
Straight		4	20
Three of a Kind		2	10
Two Pairs		1	5

*** Payback: 93.3% for 4000
94.5% for 4700
95.0% for 5000

JOKER WILD - KINGS OR BETTER

JW-09	Strategy **JWC**	1 coin	5 coins
Natural Royal Flush		400	***
Five of a Kind		200	1000
Joker Royal Flush		100	500
Straight Flush		50	250
Four of a Kind		20	100
Full House		7	35
Flush		5	25
Straight		3	15
Three of a Kind		2	10
Two Pairs		1	5
Kings or Better		1	5

*** Payback: 100.6% for 4000
101.0% for 4700
101.1% for 5000

JW-10	Strategy **JWC**	1 coin	5 coins
Natural Royal Flush		400	***
Five of a Kind		200	1000
Joker Royal Flush		100	500
Straight Flush		50	250
Four of a Kind		17	85
Full House		7	35
Flush		5	25
Straight		3	15
Three of a Kind		2	10
Two Pairs		1	5
Kings or Better		1	5

*** Payback: 98.0% for 4000
98.4% for 4700
98.5% for 5000

JOKER WILD - KINGS OR BETTER

JW-11	Strategy JWC	1 coin	5 coins
Natural Royal Flush		400	***
Five of a Kind		200	1000
Joker Royal Flush		100	500
Straight Flush		50	250
Four of a Kind		15	75
Full House		8	40
Flush		5	25
Straight		3	15
Three of a Kind		2	10
Two Pairs		1	5
Kings or Better		1	5

*** Payback: 97.9% for 4000
98.2% for 4700
98.4% for 5000

JW-12	Strategy JWC	1 coin	5 coins
Natural Royal Flush		400	***
Five of a Kind		200	1000
Joker Royal Flush		100	500
Straight Flush		50	250
Four of a Kind		15	75
Full House		7	35
Flush		5	25
Straight		3	15
Three of a Kind		2	10
Two Pairs		1	5
Kings or Better		1	5

*** Payback: 96.3% for 4000
96.7% for 4700
96.8% for 5000

JOKER WILD - KINGS OR BETTER

JW-13	Strategy **JWC**	1 coin	5 coins
Natural Royal Flush		400	***
Five of a Kind		200	1000
Joker Royal Flush		100	500
Straight Flush		50	250
Four of a Kind		20	100
Full House		5	25
Flush		4	20
Straight		3	15
Three of a Kind		2	10
Two Pairs		1	5
Kings or Better		1	5

*** Payback: 96.0% for 4000
96.3% for 4700
96.5% for 5000

JW-14	Strategy **JWC**	1 coin	5 coins
Natural Royal Flush		500	***
Five of a Kind		200	1000
Joker Royal Flush		100	500
Straight Flush		40	200
Four of a Kind		20	100
Full House		5	25
Flush		4	20
Straight		3	15
Three of a Kind		2	10
Two Pairs		1	5
Kings or Better		1	5

*** Payback: 95.4% for 4000
95.7% for 4700
95.9% for 5000

UNCONVENTIONAL GAMES

DEUCES AND JOKER WILD:

This game has five wild cards in a 53-card deck, with the top hand being five wild cards. If you can find one, the deuces and joker wild machines have an excellent 99% payback in Nevada casinos, but the versions found along the Mississippi pay only about 93%.

DOUBLE JOKER WILD:

Two wild jokers in a 54-card deck, with two pairs being the lowest-paying hand. There are two almost identical versions: one has an excellent payback of 100%, the other pays less than 98%.

FIVE DECK POKER:

This unique type of video poker game uses five separate decks of cards, one for each card position. Each of the five cards in the original deal comes from its own dedicated 52-card deck. On the draw, each replacement card is dealt from the same deck as was the original card in that position. As a result, it is possible to have a hand with five identical cards, such as five queens of diamonds.

DEUCES AND JOKER WILD

DJ-01	Strategy **DJA**	1 coin	5 coins
Five Wild Cards		1000	10000
Natural Royal Flush		250	4000
Four Deuces		25	125
Wild Royal Flush		12	60
Five of a Kind		9	45
Straight Flush		6	30
Four of a Kind		3	15
Full House		3	15
Flush		3	15
Straight		3	15
Three of a Kind		1	5
Payback: 99.0%			

DJ-02	Strategy **NR**	1 coin	5 coins
Five Wild Cards		250	2500
Natural Royal Flush		400	2000
Four Deuces		100	500
Wild Royal Flush		20	100
Five of a Kind		12	60
Straight Flush		7	35
Four of a Kind		3	15
Full House		2	10
Flush		2	10
Straight		1	5
Three of a Kind		1	5
Payback: 93.0%			

DOUBLE JOKER WILD

JJ-01	Strategy JJA	1 coin	5 coins
Natural Royal Flush		250	4000
Joker Royal Flush		100	500
Five of a Kind		50	250
Straight Flush		25	125
Four of a Kind		9	45
Full House		5	25
Flush		4	20
Straight		3	15
Three of a Kind		2	10
Two Pairs		1	5

Payback: 100.0%

JJ-02	Strategy JJA	1 coin	5 coins
Natural Royal Flush		250	4000
Joker Royal Flush		100	500
Five of a Kind		50	250
Straight Flush		25	125
Four of a Kind		8	40
Full House		5	25
Flush		4	20
Straight		3	15
Three of a Kind		2	10
Two Pairs		1	5

Payback: 97.7%

FIVE DECK POKER

FD-01	Strategy **FDA**	1 coin	5 coins
Five of a Kind (same suit)		1000	10000
Royal Flush		250	4000
Straight Flush		50	250
Five of a Kind		50	250
Four of a Kind (same suit)		20	100
Full House (same suit)		12	60
Four of a Kind		10	50
Full House		6	30
Three of a Kind (same suit)		4	20
Flush		4	20
Straight		3	15
Three of a Kind		2	10
Two Pairs (same suit)		2	10
Two Pairs		1	5

Payback: 97.2%

FD-02	Strategy **FDA**	1 coin	5 coins
Five of a Kind (same suit)		1000	10000
Royal Flush		250	4000
Straight Flush		50	250
Five of a Kind		40	200
Four of a Kind (same suit)		20	100
Full House (same suit)		10	50
Four of a Kind		10	50
Full House		5	25
Three of a Kind (same suit)		4	20
Flush		4	20
Straight		3	15
Three of a Kind		2	10
Two Pairs (same suit)		2	10
Two Pairs		1	5

Payback: 95.7%

PROGRESSIVE JACKPOT

A progressive jackpot network is a group of machines that are electrically connected to a common jackpot pool. A small percentage of the money paid in by the players is diverted to the jackpot pool, which grows until someone wins it. The jackpot is then reset to a minimum value and the growth cycle repeats itself. Each player competes against all the other players on that network.

A progressive network may consist of a local bank of a dozen machines with a jackpot that rarely exceeds a few thousand dollars. The winning hand is usually a natural royal flush, so the chance of hitting the jackpot is not unreasonable.

If the machine is part of a city-wide or state-wide network that interconnects hundeds of other machines, the winning progressive hand is always a very rare kind such as a sequential royal flush. Consequently, the jackpot pool can reach a very high value.

NOTE: The progressive payouts shown here are for 25¢ machines. For $1 machines, multiply by four. The charts in this section are grouped by type: *Wide Area, Jacks or Better, Deuces Wild, and Joker Wild.*

> **TYPICAL DESCRIPTIVE NAMES:**
> • Deuces Wild
> • Jacks Or Better
> • Joker Poker
> • Megapoker (Wide Area)
> • Pokermania (Wide Area)

POKERMANIA: Progressive Sequential Royal (suited) at jackpot reset: $100,000; at 100% payback, $800,000.

Progressive Sequential Royal (unsuited) at jackpot reset: $1000; at 100% payback, $8000.

PR-01	Strategy **PRA**	1 coin	5 coins
Royal Flush		250	4000
Straight Flush		100	500
Quad Aces		160	800
Quad 2, 3, or 4		80	400
Quad 5 thru King		50	250
Full House		8	40
Flush		6	30
Straight		4	20
Three of a Kind		3	15
Two Pairs		1	5
Jacks or Better		1	5

Payback: 95.8%; at reset 95.5% w/o sequential royals.

Note: Progressive payouts are for quarter machines. For dollars, multiply by four.

POKERMANIA: Progressive Sequential Royal (suited) at jackpot reset: $100,000; at 100% payback, $800,000

Progressive Sequential Royal (unsuited) at jackpot reset: $1000; at 100% payback, $8000

PR-02	Strategy **PRB**	1 coin	5 coins
Royal Flush		250	4000
Straight Flush		50	250
Four-of-a-Kind		25	125
Full House		9	45
Flush		6	30
Straight		4	20
Three of a Kind		3	15
Two Pairs		2	10
Jacks or Better		1	5

Payback: 95.8%; at reset 95.5% w/o sequential royals.

Note: Progressive payouts are for quarter machines. For dollars, multiply by four.

MEGAPOKER: Progressive Sequential Royal at jackpot reset: $20,000; at 100% payback, $160,000.

PR-03	Strategy **PRC**	1 coin	5 coins
Royal Flush		250	4000
Straight Flush		50	250
Four-of-a-Kind		25	125
Full House		8	40
Flush		5	25
Straight		4	20
Three of a Kind		3	15
Two Pairs		2	10
Jacks or Better		1	5

Payback: 97.6%; at reset 97.3% w/o sequential royal.
Note: Progressive payouts are for quarter machines. For dollars, multiply by four.

FIVE DECK FRENZY: Progressive Five Spade Aces at jackpot reset: $200,000; at 100% payback, $540,000.

PR-04	Strategy **PRD**	1 coin	5 coins
Five of a Kind (same suit)		1000	10,000
Royal Flush		250	4000
Five of a Kind		50	250
Straight Flush		50	250
Four of a Kind (same suit)		20	100
Full House (same suit*)		12	60
Four of a Kind		10	50
Full House		6	30
Flush		4	20
Three of a Kind (same suit)		4	20
Straight		3	15
Three of a Kind		2	10
Two Pairs (same suit*)		2	10
Two Pairs		1	5

Payback: 98.2%; at reset 97.1% w/o five spade aces
* Trips and pairs can be different suits.

PR-05	Strategy **PRE**	1 coin	5 coins

Progressive Royal Flush at jackpot reset: $1250; at 100% payback, $2200.

	1 coin	5 coins
Straight Flush	50	250
Four of a Kind	25	125
Full House	8	40
Flush	5	25
Straight	4	20
Three of a Kind	3	15
Two Pairs	2	10
Jacks or Better	1	5

Payback: 97.8% at reset.

PR-06	Strategy **PRE**	1 coin	5 coins

Progressive Royal Flush at jackpot reset: $1250; at 100% payback, $3200.

	1 coin	5 coins
Straight Flush	50	250
Four of a Kind	25	125
Full House	6	30
Flush	5	25
Straight	4	20
Three of a Kind	3	15
Two Pairs	2	10
Jacks or Better	1	5

Payback: 95.5% at reset.

PROGRESSIVE - DEUCES WILD

PR-07	Strategy **PRF**	1 coin	5 coins

Progressive Natural Royal Flush at jackpot reset: $1000; at 100% payback, $1600

	1 coin	5 coins
Four Deuces	200	1000
Deuce Royal Flush	25	125
Five of a Kind	15	75
Straight Flush	9	45
Four of a Kind	4	20
Full House	4	20
Flush	3	15
Straight	2	10
Three of a Kind	1	5

Payback: 98.9% at reset

PR-08	Strategy **PRF**	1 coin	5 coins

Progressive Natural Royal Flush at jackpot reset: $1000; at 100% payback, $4000.

	1 coin	5 coins
Four Deuces	200	1000
Deuce Royal Flush	25	125
Five of a Kind	15	75
Straight Flush	9	45
Four of a Kind	4	20
Full House	3	15
Flush	2	10
Straight	2	10
Three of a Kind	1	5

Payback: 94.3% at reset

PROGRESSIVE - JOKER WILD

PR-09	Strategy **PRG**	1 coin	5 coins

Progressive Natural Royal Flush at jackpot reset: $1000; at 100% payback, $1400.

	1 coin	5 coins
Five of a Kind	100	500
Joker Royal Flush	50	250
Straight Flush	50	250
Four of a Kind	20	100
Full House	10	50
Flush	6	30
Straight	5	25
Three of a Kind	2	10
Two Pairs	1	5

Payback: 99.4% at reset

PR-10	Strategy **PRG**	1 coin	5 coins

Progressive Natural Royal Flush at jackpot reset: $1000; at 100% payback, $1800

	1 coin	5 coins
Five of a Kind	100	500
Joker Royal Flush	50	250
Straight Flush	50	250
Four of a Kind	20	100
Full House	8	40
Flush	7	35
Straight	5	25
Three of a Kind	2	10
Two Pairs	1	5

Payback: 98.6% at reset

PROGRESSIVE - JOKER WILD

PR-11	Strategy **PRH**	1 coin	5 coins

Progressive Natural Royal Flush at jackpot reset: $1000; at 100% payback, $1900

	1 coin	5 coins
Five of a Kind	250	1250
Joker Royal Flush	200	1000
Straight Flush	50	250
Four of a Kind	10	50
Full House	5	25
Flush	4	20
Straight	3	15
Three of a Kind	2	10
Two Pairs	1	5
Jacks or Better	1	5

Payback: 98.0% at reset

PR-12	Strategy **PRH**	1 coin	5 coins

Progressive Natural Royal Flush at jackpot reset: $1000; at 100% payback, $2000

	1 coin	5 coins
Five of a Kind	200	1000
Joker Royal Flush	100	500
Straight Flush	50	250
Four of a Kind	15	75
Full House	8	40
Flush	5	25
Straight	3	15
Three of a Kind	2	10
Two Pairs	1	5
Kings or Better	1	5

Payback: 97.9% at reset

PLAYING STRATEGY TABLES

Play the Maximum Coins

The one consistency in all video poker machines is that the per-coin payout for the highest hand is always enhanced when the maximum number of coins (or credits) is played. The playing strategies in this chapter are based on five-coin play, unless otherwise noted.

IMPORTANT!
Because they are so important, the strategy rules stated earlier in this book will be repeated here. These rules must be followed to assure maximum effectiveness of the playing strategy.

Many players find that $1 machines deplete their bankroll too quickly. Therefore, if you feel uneasy playing for $5 a hand, move to a quarter machine. If you insist on playing fewer than the maximum coins, be aware that the long-term payback will be reduced by 1-2%—and much more if you hit an early royal. However, there is one caution: If you move from a quarter machine to a nickel machine, be sure that the payout schedule is the same.

Although there isn't much variation in schedules between quarter, dollar, and five-dollar machines, most nickel machines have significantly poorer payout schedules.

Never Hold a Kicker

A kicker is an unmatched card held in the hand when drawing replacement cards. Holding a kicker is disastrous because it significantly reduces the chances of improving a hand. For instance, on a full-pay jacks-or-better machine, keeping a kicker with a high pair reduces the overall payback by over 1.5 percent. If you are dealt a low pair, discarding two instead of three cards reduces the payback by almost four percent. Don't do it.

Stick to the Strategy

Do not try to outguess the strategy table. The table is based on mathematical probabilities and your hunch is not. Once in a while you may guess correctly, but over the long run the strategy table will serve you well. If you don't like the idea of breaking a straight or a flush in order to draw one card to a possible royal, maybe you are playing the wrong game.

Do not depend on your memory

Take this book into the casino and refer to it frequently. Many of the differences between the various strategy tables are quite subtle. Until you are familiar with a particular version of video poker don't depend too much on your memory. For instance, if you are not absolutely sure what to do when your hand contains four cards to a flush along with a pair of kings, be sure to open the book. After you have played a particular game for a while, you will get to know the strategy by heart.

Quit when you are ahead

This rule actually falls in the category of money management, but it is so important that it should be a part of the overall playing strategy. When you hit a jackpot or a good bonus payout, that is a good time to quit for a while. Experience has shown that with continued play, the chances are that you will fritter away the winnings, and that is what the casinos depend on.

NOTES ON STRAIGHTS AND STRAIGHT FLUSHES

Straights and straight flushes come in several flavors. Incomplete straights and straight flushes are modified by the terms *outside*, *inside*, and *single-ended*. *Single-ended* means that an incomplete straight or straight flush has no gap but has an ace, either at the low or the high end. *Inside* means that there is a gap in the sequence. *Outside* means that there is no gap and adding a card at either end can complete the straight or straight flush. Since they are statistically the same, the term "inside" will be used to designate both single-ended and inside varieties.

In the strategy tables, if a 4-card straight or straight flush does *not* have a modifier, it may be either inside (or single-ended) or outside. If the modifier *outside* is used, then it can only be an outside straight or straight flush. If the modifier *inside* is used, it can only be inside or single-ended. By the same reasoning, a 3-card outside straight can have no gaps in the sequence.

NOTES ON HIGH CARD

The meaning of High Card or HC depends on the particular game, as follows:

- In Tens-or-Better it means:
  ten, jack, queen, king, or ace.
- In Jacks-or-Better it means:
  jack, queen, king, or ace.
- In Kings-or-Better:
  it means king or ace.

NOTES ON WILD-CARD GAMES

The wild-card games have more than one strategy list, since the strategy depends on the number of wild cards in the initial deal. For instance, if the initial hand contains two deuces, use the strategy listing under "TWO DEUCE HAND."

SPECIAL TERMS

The strategy tables contain some terminology that may be unfamiliar. These terms are explained below:

Sequential

This means that the cards making up a royal flush have to appear on the video screen in sequential order, such as 10-J-Q-K-A. The sequence may start with a ten or with an ace, depending on how it is defined by the particular machine.

Non-Sequential

This term is used to clearly differentiate from the sequential requirement. It means that the cards may appear in any order.

Suited

This means that all the cards in a royal flush or straight flush have to be of the specific suit pre-defined by the particular machine you are playing.

APPLYING THE PLAYING STRATEGY

After finding the matching payout chart in the Payout Schedules chapter, note the strategy code and turn to the indicated strategy table in this chapter. Each strategy table lists all possible pre-draw hands in the order they should be played. After the initial five cards are dealt, work your way down from the top of the strategy table until you find a match and then draw the indicated number of cards.

You do not have to consult the strategy table for every hand that is dealt. For most hands, the correct strategy is obvious. The main purpose of the table is to resolve conflicts when there is more than one way to logically play a hand. For instance, what do you do if you are dealt a pat flush that includes a four-card royal? What about a four-flush that includes a three-card royal? Once you have learned these things, remember to recheck the strategy table whenever you play a new type of game.

The following strategy tables are arranged in alphabetical order by strategy code.

BONUS QUADS
STRATEGY TABLE BQA

DEALT HAND	DRAW
Royal Flush	0
Straight Flush	0
4 of a Kind	0
4-Card Royal Flush	1
Full House	0
4-Card Outside Straight Flush	1
Flush	0
3 of a Kind	2
Straight	0
4-Card Inside Straight Flush	1
2 Pairs	1
Pair J, Q, K, or A	3
3-Card Royal Flush	2
4-Card Flush	1
9-10-J (same suit)	2
4-Card Outside Straight (1 to 3 HC)	1
Pair 2 thru 10	3
3-Card Straight Flush	2
4-Card Outside Straight	1
J-Q-K-A (mixed suits)	1
2-Card Royal Flush	3
J-Q-K (mixed suits)	2
1 or 2 High Cards	3-4
Mixed Low Cards	5

BONUS QUADS
STRATEGY TABLE BQB

DEALT HAND	DRAW
Royal Flush	0
Straight Flush	0
4 of a Kind	0
4-Card Royal Flush	1
3 Deuces	2
Full House	0
Flush	0
3 of a Kind	2
Straight	0
2 Pairs	1
4-Card Straight Flush	1
Pair J, Q, K, or A	3
3-Card Royal Flush	2
4-Card Flush	1
Pair 2 thru 10	3
4-Card Outside Straight (1 to 3 HC)	1
9-10-J (same suit)	2
4-Card Outside Straight	1
3-Card Straight Flush	2
J-Q-K-A (mixed suits)	1
2-Card Royal Flush	3
J-Q-K (mixed suits)	2
1 or 2 High Cards	3-4
Mixed Low Cards	5

BONUS QUADS
STRATEGY TABLE BQC

DEALT HAND	DRAW
Royal Flush	0
Straight Flush	0
4 of a Kind	0
4-Card Royal Flush	1
Full House	0
Flush	0
3 of a Kind	2
Straight	0
2 Pairs	1
4-Card Straight Flush	1
Pair J, Q, K, or A	3
3-Card Royal Flush	2
4-Card Flush	1
Pair 2 thru 10	3
4-Card Outside Straight (1 to 3 HC)	1
9-10-J (same suit)	2
4-Card Outside Straight	1
3-Card Straight Flush	2
J-Q-K-A (mixed suits)	1
2-Card Royal Flush	3
J-Q-K (mixed suits)	2
1 or 2 High Cards	3-4
Mixed Low Cards	5

BONUS QUADS
STRATEGY TABLE BQD

DEALT HAND	DRAW
Royal Flush	0
Straight Flush	0
4 of a Kind	0
Flush	0
4-Card Royal Flush	1
3 Aces	2
Full House	0
3 of a Kind	2
4-Card Straight Flush	1
4-Card Flush	1
Straight	0
3-Card Royal Flush	2
Pair Aces	3
2 Pairs	1
Pair J, Q, or K	3
3-Card Straight Flush	2
3-Card Flush	2
Pair 2 thru 10	3
2-Card Royal Flush	3
4-Card Outside Straight (1 to 3 HC)	1
4-Card Outside Straight	1
1 Ace	4
1, 2, or 3 High Cards	2-3-4
2-Card Flush	3
Mixed Low Cards	5

BONUS QUADS
STRATEGY TABLE BQE

DEALT HAND	DRAW
Royal Flush	0
Straight Flush	0
4 of a Kind	0
4-Card Royal Flush	1
3 Aces	2
Full House	0
Flush	0
3 of a Kind	2
Straight	0
4-Card Straight Flush	1
2 Pairs	1
Pair J, Q, K, or A	3
3-Card Royal Flush	2
4-Card Flush	1
4-Card Outside Straight	1
Pair 2 thru 10	3
9-10-J (same suit)	2
3-Card Straight Flush	2
J-Q-K-A (mixed suits)	1
J-Q-K (mixed suits)	2
10-J-Q (mixed suits)	2
2-Card Royal Flush	3
4-Card Inside Straight	1
1 or 2 High Cards	3-4
3-Card Flush	2
Mixed Low Cards	5

BONUS QUADS
STRATEGY TABLE BQF

DEALT HAND	DRAW
Royal Flush	0
Straight Flush	0
4 of a Kind	0
4-Card Royal Flush	1
3 Aces	2
Full House	0
3 of a Kind	2
Flush	0
Straight	0
4-Card Straight Flush	1
Pair Aces	3
2 Pairs	1
Pair Kings	3
4-Card Flush	1
3-Card Royal Flush	2
Pair 2 thru Q	3
10-J-Q-K (mixed suits)	1
4-Card Outside Straight	1
3-Card Straight Flush	2
Ace and/or King	3-4
4-Card Inside Straight	1
Mixed Low Cards	5

BONUS QUADS
STRATEGY TABLE BQG

DEALT HAND	DRAW
Royal Flush	0
Straight Flush	0
4 of a Kind	0
3 Aces	2
4-Card Royal Flush	1
Full House	0
3 of a Kind	2
Flush	0
Straight	0
4-Card Outside Straight Flush	1
Pair Aces	3
4-Card Inside Straight Flush	1
2 Pairs	1
Pair J, Q, or K	3
3-Card Royal Flush	2
4-Card Flush	1
4-Card Outside Straight	1
Pair 2 thru 10	3
9-10-J (same suit)	2
J-Q-K-A (mixed suits)	1
3-Card Straight Flush	2
2-Card Royal Flush	3
J-Q-K (mixed suits)	2
1 Ace	4
4-Card Inside Straight	1
1 or 2 High Cards	3-4
Mixed Low Cards	5

BONUS QUADS
STRATEGY TABLE BQH

DEALT HAND	DRAW
Royal Flush	0
Straight Flush	0
4 of a Kind	0
4-Card Royal Flush	1
3 Aces	2
Full House	0
Flush	0
3 of a Kind	2
Straight	0
4-Card Straight Flush	1
Pair Aces	3
2 Pairs	1
3-Card Royal Flush	2
Pair J, Q, or K	3
4-Card Flush	1
Pair 2, 3, or 4	3
4-Card Outside Straight (1 to 3 HC)	1
Pair 5 thru 10	3
9-10-J (same suit)	2
4-Card Outside Straight	1
J-Q-K-A (mixed suits)	1
3-Card Straight Flush	2
2-Card Royal Flush	3
J-Q-K (mixed suits)	2
1 or 2 High Cards	3-4
4-Card Inside Straight	1
Mixed Low Cards	5

BONUS ROYALS
STRATEGY TABLE BRA

DEALT HAND	DRAW
Royal Flush	0
Straight Flush	0
4 of a Kind	0
4-Card Royal Flush	1
Flush (suited)	0
Full House	0
4-Card Outside Straight Flush(suited)	1
Flush	0
3 of a Kind	2
4-Card Inside Straight Flush (suited)	1
Straight	0
4-Card Outside Straight Flush	1
3-Card Royal Flush (suited)	2
2 Pairs	1
4-Card Inside Straight Flush	1
4-Card Flush (suited)	1
3-Card Royal Flush	2
Pair J, Q, K, or A	3
4-Card Flush	1
3-Card Straight Flush (suited)	2
Pair 2 thru 10	3
4-Card Outside Straight	1
2-Card Royal Flush (suited)	3
3-Card Straight Flush	2
J-Q-K-A (mixed suits)	1
J-Q-K (mixed suits)	2
2-Card Royal Flush	3
1 or 2 High Cards	3-4
Mixed Low Cards	5

BONUS ROYALS
STRATEGY TABLE BRB

DEALT HAND	DRAW
Royal Flush	0
Straight Flush	0
4 of a Kind	0
4-Card Royal Flush (seq or non-seq)	1
3 Aces	2
Full House	0
Flush	0
3 of a Kind	2
Straight	0
4-Card Straight Flush	1
3-Card Sequential Royal Flush	2
Pair Aces	3
2 Pairs	1
3-Card Non-Seq Royal Flush	2
Pair J, Q, or K	3
4-Card Flush	1
Pair 2, 3, or 4	3
4-Card Outside Straight (1 to 3 HC)	1
Pair 5 thru 10	3
4-Card Outside Straight	1
J-Q-K-A (mixed suits)	1
3-Card Straight Flush	2
2-Card Royal Flush	3
J-Q-K (mixed suits)	2
1 or 2 High Cards	3-4
Mixed Low Cards	5

BONUS ROYALS
STRATEGY TABLE BRC

DEALT HAND	DRAW
Royal Flush	0
Low Royal Flush (2 thru 6)	0
Straight Flush	0
4 of a Kind	0
4-Card Royal Flush	1
4-Card Lo Royal Flush	1
Full House	0
Flush	0
3 of a Kind	2
Straight	0
4-Card Straight Flush	1
2 Pairs	1
Pair J, Q, K, or A	3
3-Card Royal Flush	2
3-Card Lo Royal Flush	2
4-Card Flush	1
4-Card Outside Straight (1 to 3 HC)	1
Pair 2 thru 10	3
4-Card Outside Straight	1
3-Card Straight Flush	2
2-Card Royal Flush (high)	3
J-Q-K-A (mixed suits)	1
J-Q-K (mixed suits)	1
1 or 2 High Cards	3-4
Mixed Low Cards	5

DEUCES AND JOKER WILD STRATEGY TABLE DJA

DEALT HAND	DRAW
NO WILD CARDS	
Natural Royal Flush	0
4-Card Royal Flush	1
Straight Flush	0
4 of a Kind	1
Full House	0
Flush	0
Straight	0
3 of a Kind	2
4-Card Straight Flush	1
3-Card Royal Flush	2
4-Card Flush	1
3-Card Straight Flush	2
2 Pairs	1
1 Pair	3
4-Card Straight	1
Assorted Cards	5
ONE WILD CARD	
Royal Flush	0
5 of a Kind	0
Straight Flush	0
4 of a Kind	1
Full House	0
Flush	0
4-Card Royal Flush	1
Straight	0
4-Card Straight Flush	1
3 of a Kind	2
3-Card Straight Flush	2

DEALT HAND	DRAW
ONE WILD CARD (cont'd)	
3-Card Royal Flush	2
4-Card Straight	1
4-Card Flush	1
1 Wild Card	4
TWO WILD CARDS	
Royal Flush	0
5 of a Kind	0
Straight Flush	0
4 of a Kind	1
4-Card Royal Flush	1
Flush	0
4-Card Straight Flush	1
2 Wild Cards	3
THREE WILD CARDS	
Royal Flush	0
5 of a Kind	0
3 Wild Cards	2
FOUR WILD CARDS	
4 Deuces	1
3 Deuces and Joker	1
FIVE WILD CARDS	
5 Wild Cards	0

DEUCES WILD
STRATEGY TABLE DWA

DEALT HAND	DRAW
NO DEUCES	
Natural Royal Flush	0
4-Card Royal Flush	1
Straight Flush	0
4 of a Kind	1
Full House	0
3 of a Kind	2
Flush	0
Straight	0
4-Card Straight Flush	1
3-Card Royal Flush	2
1 Pair (discard 2nd pair)	3
4-Card Outside Straight	1
4-Card Flush	1
3-Card Straight Flush	2
2-Card Royal (J or Q high)	3
Assorted Cards	5
ONE DEUCE HAND	
Royal Flush	0
5 of a Kind	0
Straight Flush	0
4 of a Kind	1
4-Card Royal Flush	1
Full House	0
3 of a Kind	2
4-Card Straight Flush	1
Flush	0
Straight	0
3-Card Royal Flush	2
1 Deuce	4

DEUCES WILD
STRATEGY TABLE DWA
continued

DEALT HAND   **DRAW**

TWO DEUCE HAND

Royal Flush	0
5 of a Kind	0
Straight Flush	0
4 of a Kind	1
4-Card Royal Flush	1
2 Deuces	3

THREE DEUCE HAND

Royal Flush	0
5 of a Kind	0
3 Deuces	2

FOUR DEUCE HAND

4 Deuces	1

DEUCES WILD
STRATEGY TABLE DWB

DEALT HAND	DRAW
NO DEUCES	
Natural Royal Flush	0
4-Card Royal Flush	1
Straight Flush	0
4 of a Kind	1
Full House	0
Flush	0
Straight	0
3 of a Kind	2
4-Card Straight Flush	1
3-Card Royal Flush	2
4-Card Flush	1
2 Pairs	1
1 Pair	3
4-Card Outside Straight	1
3-Card Straight Flush	2
2-Card Royal Flush	3
Assorted Cards	5
ONE DEUCE HAND	
Royal Flush	0
5 of a Kind	0
Straight Flush	0
4 of a Kind	1
Full House	0
4-Card Royal Flush	1
Flush	0
4-Card Straight Flush	1
Straight	0
3 of a Kind	2
3-Card Royal Flush	2
3-Card OutsideStraight Flush	2
1 Deuce	4

DEUCES WILD
STRATEGY TABLE DWB
continued

DEALT HAND	DRAW
TWO DEUCE HAND	
Royal Flush	0
5 of a Kind	0
Straight Flush	0
4 of a Kind	1
4-Card Royal Flush	1
4-Card Straight Flush	1
2 Deuces	3
THREE DEUCE HAND	
Royal Flush	0
5 of a Kind	0
3 Deuces	2
FOUR DEUCE HAND	
4 Deuces	1

DEUCES WILD
STRATEGY TABLE DWC

DEALT HAND	DRAW
NO DEUCES	
Natural Royal Flush	0
4-Card Royal Flush	1
Straight Flush	0
4 of a Kind	1
Full House	0
Flush	0
Straight	0
3 of a Kind	2
4-Card Straight Flush	1
3-Card Royal Flush	2
3-Card Outside Straight Flush	2
1 Pair (discard 2nd pair)	3
4-Card Outside Straight	1
4-Card Flush	1
3-Card Inside Straight Flush	2
2-Card Royal Flush	3
Assorted Cards	5
ONE DEUCE HAND	
Royal Flush	0
5 of a Kind	0
Straight Flush	0
4 of a Kind	1
4-Card Royal Flush	1
Full House	0
4-Card Straight Flush	1
Flush	0
Straight	0
3 of a Kind	2
3-Card Royal Flush	2
3-Card Straight Flush	2
1 Deuce	4

DEUCES WILD
STRATEGY TABLE DWC
continued

DEALT HAND	DRAW
TWO DEUCE HAND	
Royal Flush	0
5 of a Kind	0
Straight Flush	0
4 of a Kind	1
4-Card Royal Flush	1
2 Deuces	3
THREE DEUCE HAND	
Royal Flush	0
5 of a Kind	0
3 Deuces	2
FOUR DEUCE HAND	
4 Deuces	1

DEUCES WILD
STRATEGY TABLE DWD

DEALT HAND	DRAW
NO DEUCES	
Natural Royal Flush	0
4-Card Royal Flush	1
Straight Flush	0
4 of a Kind	1
Full House	0
Flush	0
Straight	0
3 of a Kind	2
4-Card Straight Flush	1
3-Card Royal Flush	2
4-Card Flush	1
2 Pairs	1
1 Pair	3
4-Card Outside Straight	1
3-Card Straight Flush	2
2-Card Royal (no Ace)	3
Assorted Cards	5
ONE DEUCE HAND	
Royal Flush	0
5 of a Kind	0
Straight Flush	0
4 of a Kind	1
Full House	0
4-Card Royal Flush	1
Flush	0
4-Card Straight Flush	1
Straight	0
3 of a Kind	2
3-Card Royal Flush	2
1 Deuce	4

DEUCES WILD
STRATEGY TABLE DWD
continued

DEALT HAND	DRAW
TWO DEUCE HAND	
Royal Flush	0
5 of a Kind	0
Straight Flush	0
4 of a Kind	1
4-Card Royal Flush	1
2 Deuces	3
THREE DEUCE HAND	
Royal Flush	0
3 Deuces	2
FOUR DEUCE HAND	
4 Deuces	1

DEUCES WILD
STRATEGY TABLE DWE

DEALT HAND	DRAW
NO DEUCES	
Natural Royal Flush	0
4-Card Royal Flush	1
Straight Flush	0
4 of a Kind	1
Full House	0
Flush	0
Straight	0
3 of a Kind	2
4-Card Straight Flush	1
3-Card Royal Flush	2
1 Pair (discard 2nd pair)	3
4-Card Outside Straight	1
4-Card Flush	1
3-Card Straight Flush	2
2-Card Royal (J or Q high)	3
Assorted Cards	5
ONE DEUCE HAND	
Royal Flush	0
5 of a Kind	0
Straight Flush	0
4 of a Kind	1
4-Card Royal Flush	1
Full House	0
4-Card Straight Flush	1
Flush	0
Straight	0
3 of a Kind	2
3-Card Royal Flush (no Ace)	2
1 Deuce	4

DEALT HAND	DRAW

TWO DEUCE HAND

Royal Flush	0
5 of a Kind	0
Straight Flush	0
4 of a Kind	1
4-Card Royal Flush	1
2 Deuces	3

THREE DEUCE HAND

Royal Flush	0
3 Deuces	2

FOUR DEUCE HAND

4 Deuces	1

FIVE DECK POKER
STRATEGY TABLE FDA

DEALT HAND	DRAW
5 of a Kind (same suit)	0
Royal Flush	0
4 of a Kind (same suit)	1
5 of a Kind	0
Straight Flush	0
4-Card Royal Flush	1
4 of a Kind	1
Full House	0
3 of a Kind (same suit)	2
Flush	0
3 of a Kind	2
4-Card Outside Straight Flush	1
Straight	0
2 Pairs (each pair same suit)	1
4-Card Inside Straight Flush	1
2 Pairs	1
3-Card Royal Flush	2
4-Card Flush	1
Any Pair	3
3-Card Straight Flush	2
4-Card Outside Straight	1
3-Card Flush	2
2-Card Royal Flush	3
2-card Straight Flush	3
Mixed Low Cards	5

ORIGINAL JACKS OR BETTER STRATEGY TABLE JBA

DEALT HAND	DRAW
Royal Flush	0
Straight Flush	0
4 of a Kind	0
4-Card Royal Flush	1
Full House	0
Flush	0
3 of a Kind	2
Straight	0
2 Pairs	1
4-Card Straight Flush	1
Pair J, Q, K, or A	3
3-Card Royal Flush	2
4-Card Flush	1
Pair 2 thru 10	3
4-Card Outside Straight	1
3-Card Straight Flush	2
J-Q, J-K, or Q-K (same suit)	3
4-Card Inside Straight (3 or 4 HC)	1
J-A, Q-A, or K-A (same suit)	3
J-Q-K (mixed suits)	2
10-J, 10-Q, or 10-K (same suit)	3
1 or 2 High Cards	3-4
Mixed Low Cards	5

ORIGINAL JACKS OR BETTER
STRATEGY TABLE JBB

<u>DEALT HAND</u>	<u>DRAW</u>
Royal Flush	0
Straight Flush	0
4 of a Kind	0
4-Card Royal Flush	1
4-Card Outside Straight Flush	1
Full House	0
Flush	0
Straight	0
4-Card Inside Straight Flush	1
3 of a Kind	2
3-Card Royal Flush	2
2 Pairs	1
4-Card Flush	1
4-Card Outside Straight	1
Pair J, Q, K, or A	3
3-Card Straight Flush	2
4-Card Inside Straight	1
Pair 2 thru 10	3
J-Q, J-K, or Q-K (same suit)	3
3-Card Outside Straight (1 to 3 HC)	2
2-Card Royal Flush	3
3-Card Flush	2
1 or 2 High Cards	3-4
3-Card Straight	2
2-Card Straight Flush	3
Mixed Low Cards	5

DOUBLE JOKER WILD
STRATEGY TABLE JJA

DEALT HAND	DRAW
NO JOKER	
Natural Royal Flush	0
Straight Flush	0
4-Card Royal Flush	1
4 of a Kind	1
Full House	0
Flush	0
Straight	0
3 of a Kind	2
4-Card Straight Flush	1
2 Pairs	1
3-Card Royal Flush	2
4-Card Flush	1
Any Pair	3
4-Card Outside Straight	1
3-Card Straight Flush	2
4-Card Inside Straight	1
2-Card Royal Flush	3
Assorted Cards	5

continued on next page

ONE JOKER HAND

Royal Flush 0
5 of a Kind 0
Straight Flush 0
4 of a Kind 1
4-Card Royal Flush 1
Full House 0
Flush 0
4-Card Straight Flush 1
Straight 0
3 of a Kind 2
3-Card Royal Flush 2
3-Card Straight Flush 2
4-Card Outside Straight 1
4-Card Flush 1
Joker 4

TWO JOKER HAND

Royal Flush 0
5 of a Kind 0
Straight Flush 0
4 of a Kind 1
4-Card Royal Flush 1
4-Card Straight Flush 1
2 Jokers 3

DEALT HAND	DRAW
NO JOKER	
Natural Royal Flush	0
Straight Flush	0
4-Card Royal Flush	1
4 of a Kind	1
Full House	0
Flush	0
Straight	0
4-Card Straight Flush	1
3 of a Kind	2
2 Pairs	1
3-Card Royal Flush	2
4-Card Flush	1
4-Card Outside Straight	1
3-Card Straight Flush	2
1 Pair	3
4-Card Inside Straight	1
3-Card Flush	2
2-Card Royal Flush	3
3-Card Outside Straight	2
2-Card Straight Flush	3
Assorted Cards	5

continued on next page

DEALT HAND	DRAW
JOKER HAND	
5 of a Kind	0
Royal Flush	0
Straight Flush	0
4 of a Kind	1
Full House	0
Flush	0
4-Card Royal Flush	1
4-Card Straight Flush	1
Straight	0
3 of a Kind	2
3-Card Straight Flush	2
4-Card Flush	1
4-Card Straight	1
3-Card Outside Straight	2
Joker	4

JOKER WILD - TWO PAIRS
STRATEGY TABLE JWB

DEALT HAND	DRAW
NO JOKER	
Natural Royal Flush	0
Straight Flush	0
4 of a Kind	1
Full House	0
4-Card Royal Flush	1
4-Card Straight Flush	1
Flush	0
3 of a Kind	2
Straight	0
2 Pairs	1
4-Card Flush	1
3-Card Royal Flush	2
3-Card Straight Flush	2
4-Card Outside Straight	1
1 Pair	3
4-Card Inside Straight	1
2-Card Royal (no Ace)	3
3-Card Flush	2
2-Card Straight Flush	3
3-Card Outside Straight	2
Assorted Cards	5

continued on next page

DEALT HAND	DRAW
JOKER HAND	
5 of a Kind	0
Royal Flush	0
Straight Flush	0
4 of a Kind	1
4-Card Royal Flush	1
4-Card Straight Flush	1
Full House	0
Flush	0
Straight	0
3 of a Kind	2
3-Card Straight Flush	2
4-Card Outside Straight	1
4-Card Flush	1
4-Card Inside Straight	1
Joker	4

JOKER WILD - TWO PAIRS
STRATEGY TABLE JWC

DEALT HAND	DRAW

NO JOKER

Natural Royal Flush	0
Straight Flush	0
4 of a Kind	1
4-Card Royal Flush	1
Full House	0
Flush	0
3 of a Kind	2
4-Card Straight Flush	1
Straight	0
2 Pairs	1
3-Card Royal Flush	2
Pair King or Ace	3
4-Card Flush	1
Pair 2 thru Queen	3
3-Card Straight Flush	2
4-Card Outside Straight	1
2-Card Royal Flush	3
Ace and/or King	3-4
Assorted Cards	5

continued on next page

DEALT HAND	DRAW
JOKER HAND	
5 of a Kind	0
Royal Flush	0
Straight Flush	0
4 of a Kind	1
Full House	0
4-Card Royal Flush	1
Flush	0
4-Card Straight Flush	1
3 of a Kind	2
Straight	0
4-Card Flush (1 or 2 HC)	1
3-Card Royal Flush	2
3-Card Straight Flush	2
Pair King or Ace	3
4-Card Outside Straight	1
4-Card Flush	1
Joker	4

PROGRESSIVE - POKERMANIA
STRATEGY TABLE PRA

DEALT HAND	DRAW
Sequential Royal Flush (suited)	0
4-Card Seq Royal Flush (suited)	1
Royal Flush	0
Straight Flush	0
4 of a Kind	0
3-Card Seq Royal Flush (suited)	2
4-Card Royal Flush	1
3 Aces	2
Full House	0
Flush	0
4-Card Outside Straight Flush	1
3 of a Kind	2
Straight	0
4-Card Inside Straight Flush	1
Pair Aces	3
2 Pairs	1
3-Card Royal Flush	2
Pair J, Q, or K	3
2-Card Seq Royal Flush (suited)	3
4-Card Flush	1
9-10-J (same suit)	2
Pair 2 thru 10	3
3-Card Straight Flush	2
4-Card Outside Straight	1
2-Card Seq Royal Flush (J-Q or Q-K)	3
J-Q-K-A (mixed suits)	1
2-Card Royal Flush	3
J-Q-K (mixed suits)	2
1-Card Seq Royal Flush (suited)	4
1 or 2 High Cards	3-4
Mixed Low Cards	5

PROGRESSIVE - POKERMANIA
STRATEGY TABLE PRB

DEALT HAND	DRAW
Sequential Royal Flush (suited)	0
4-Card Seq Royal Flush (suited)	1
Royal Flush	0
Straight Flush	0
3-Card Seq Royal Flush (suited)	2
4 of a Kind	0
4-Card Royal Flush	1
Full House	0
Flush	0
4-Card Outside Straight Flush	1
3 of a Kind	2
Straight	0
4-Card Inside Straight Flush	1
2 Pairs	1
3-Card Royal Flush	2
Pair J, Q, K, or A	3
2-Card Seq Royal Flush (suited)	3
4-Card Flush	1
9-10-J (same suit)	2
Pair 2 thru 10	3
3-Card Straight Flush	2
4-Card Outside Straight	1
2-Card Seq Royal Flush (J-Q or Q-K)	3
J-Q-K-A (mixed suits)	1
2-Card Royal Flush	3
J-Q-K (mixed suits)	2
1-Card Seq Royal Flush (suited)	4
1 or 2 High Cards	3-4
Mixed Low Cards	5

PROGRESSIVE - MEGAPOKER STRATEGY TABLE PRC

DEALT HAND	DRAW
Sequential Royal Flush	0
4-Card Seq Royal Flush	1
Royal Flush	0
Straight Flush	0
4 of a Kind	0
3-Card Seq Royal Flush	2
4-Card Royal Flush	1
Full House	0
Flush	0
3 of a Kind	2
Straight	0
4-Card Straight Flush	1
2 Pairs	1
Pair J, Q, K, or A	3
3-Card Royal Flush	2
2-Card Seq Royal Flush	3
4-Card Flush	1
4-Card Outside Straight (1 to 3 HC)	1
Pair 2 thru 10	3
9-10-J (same suit)	2
4-Card Outside Straight	1
3-Card Straight Flush	2
J-Q-K-A (mixed suits)	1
2-Card Royal Flush	3
J-Q-K (mixed suits)	2
1 or 2 High Cards	3-4
Mixed Low Cards	5

DEALT HAND	DRAW
5 Spade Aces	0
4 Spade Aces	1
5 of a Kind (same suit)	0
Royal Flush	0
3 Spade Aces	2
4 of a Kind (same suit)	1
5 of a Kind	0
Straight Flush	0
4-Card Royal Flush	1
4 of a Kind	1
Full House	0
3 of a Kind (same suit)	2
Flush	0
3 of a Kind	2
4-Card Outside Straight Flush	1
Straight	0
2 Pairs (each pair same suit)	1
2 Spade Aces	3
4-Card Inside Straight Flush	1
2 Pairs	1
3-Card Royal Flush	2
4-Card Flush	1
Any Pair	3
3-Card Straight Flush	2
4-Card Outside Straight	1
3-Card Flush	2
2-Card Royal Flush	3
1 Spade Ace	4
2-card Straight Flush	3
Mixed Low Cards	5

DEALT HAND	DRAW
Royal Flush	0
Straight Flush	0
4-Card Royal Flush	1
4 of a Kind	0
Full House	0
Flush	0
3 of a Kind	2
Straight	0
4-Card Straight Flush	1
2 Pairs	1
3-Card Royal Flush	2
Pair J, Q, K, or A	3
4-Card Flush	1
4-Card Outside Straight (1 to 3 HC)	1
Pair 2 thru 10	3
9-10-J (same suit)	2
4-Card Outside Straight	1
2-Card Royal Flush	3
3-Card Straight Flush	2
J-Q-K-A (mixed suits)	1
J-Q-K (mixed suits)	2
1 or 2 High Cards	3-4
Mixed Low Cards	5

PROGRESSIVE - DEUCES WILD
STRATEGY TABLE PRF

DEALT HAND	DRAW
NO DEUCES	
Natural Royal Flush	0
4-Card Royal Flush	1
Straight Flush	0
4 of a Kind	1
Full House	0
Flush	0
Straight	0
3 of a Kind	2
4-Card Straight Flush	1
3-Card Royal Flush	2
4-Card Flush	1
2 Pairs	1
1 Pair	3
4-Card Outside Straight	1
3-Card Straight Flush	2
2-Card Royal	3
Assorted Cards	5
ONE DEUCE HAND	
Royal Flush	0
5 of a Kind	0
Straight Flush	0
4 of a Kind	1
Full House	0
4-Card Royal Flush	1
Flush	0
4-Card Straight Flush	1
Straight	0
3 of a Kind	2
3-Card Royal Flush	2
3-Card Outside Straight Flush	2
1 Deuce	4

PROGRESSIVE - DEUCES WILD STRATEGY TABLE PRF
continued

DEALT HAND	DRAW
TWO DEUCE HAND	
Royal Flush	0
5 of a Kind	0
Straight Flush	0
4 of a Kind	1
4-Card Royal Flush	1
4-Card Outside Straight Flush	1
2 Deuces	3
THREE DEUCE HAND	
Royal Flush	0
5 of a Kind	0
3 Deuces	2
FOUR DEUCE HAND	
4 Deuces	1

PROGRESSIVE - JOKER WILD
STRATEGY TABLE PRG

DEALT HAND	DRAW
NO JOKER	
Natural Royal Flush	0
Straight Flush	0
4-Card Royal Flush	1
4 of a Kind	1
Full House	0
Flush	0
Straight	0
4-Card Straight Flush	1
3 of a Kind	2
2 Pairs	1
3-Card Royal Flush	2
4-Card Flush	1
4-Card Outside Straight	1
3-Card Straight Flush	2
1 Pair	3
J-Q-K-A (mixed suits)	1
3-Card Flush	2
2-Card Royal Flush	3
3-Card Outside Straight	2
2-Card Straight Flush	3
Assorted Cards	5

DEALT HAND	DRAW
JOKER HAND	
5 of a Kind	0
Royal Flush	0
Straight Flush	0
4 of a Kind	1
Full House	0
Flush	0
4-Card Royal Flush	1
4-Card Straight Flush	1
Straight	0
3 of a Kind	2
3-Card Straight Flush	2
4-Card Flush	1
4-Card Straight	1
3-Card Outside Straight	2
Joker	4

DEALT HAND	DRAW
NO JOKER	
Natural Royal Flush	0
Straight Flush	0
4 of a Kind	1
4-Card Royal Flush	1
Full House	0
Flush	0
3 of a Kind	2
4-Card Straight Flush	1
Straight	0
2 Pairs	1
3-Card Royal Flush	2
4-Card Flush	1
Any Pair	3
3-Card Straight Flush	2
4-Card Outside Straight	1
2-Card Royal Flush	3
1 or 2 High Cards	3-4
Assorted Cards	5

continued on next page

DEALT HAND	DRAW
JOKER HAND	
5 of a Kind	0
Royal Flush	0
Straight Flush	0
4 of a Kind	1
4-Card Royal Flush	1
Full House	0
Flush	0
4-Card Straight Flush	1
3 of a Kind	2
Straight	0
4-Card Flush (1 or 2 HC)	1
3-Card Royal Flush	2
3-Card Straight Flush	2
High Pair	3
4-Card Outside Straight	1
4-Card Flush	1
Joker	4

TENS OR BETTER
STRATEGY TABLE TBA

DEALT HAND	DRAW
Royal Flush	0
Straight Flush	0
4 of a Kind	0
4-Card Royal Flush	1
Full House	0
Flush	0
3 of a Kind	2
Straight	0
4-Card Straight Flush	1
2 Pairs	1
3-Card Royal Flush	2
Pair J, Q, K, or A	3
4-Card Flush	1
4-Card Outside Straight (1 to 3 HC)	1
9-10-J (same suit)	2
Pair 2 thru 9	3
8-9-10 (same suit)	2
4-Card Outside Straight	1
3-Card Straight Flush	2
2-Card Royal Flush	3
J-Q-K-A (mixed suits)	1
J-Q-K (mixed suits)	2
10-J-Q (mixed suits)	2
1 or 2 High Cards	3-4
Mixed Low Cards	5

TWO PAIRS OR BETTER
STRATEGY TABLE TPA

DEALT HAND	DRAW
Royal Flush	0
Straight Flush	0
4 of a Kind	0
4-Card Royal Flush	1
Full House	0
Flush	0
4-Card Outside Straight Flush	1
Straight	0
3 of a Kind	2
4-Card Inside Straight Flush	1
2 Pairs	1
4-Card Flush	1
3-Card Royal Flush	2
4-Card Outside Straight	1
Any Pair	3
3-Card Straight Flush	2
4-Card Inside Straight	1
3-Card Flush	2
2-Card Royal Flush	3
3-Card Outside Straight	2
2-Card Straight Flush	3
2-Card Flush	3
Mixed Low Cards	5

SHORT TERM PAYBACK CORRECTION TABLES

The application of the best strategies given in this book (or any other book) doesn't guarantee a net gain for the player. This is because the strategies and overall payback percentages are based on *long-term* play.

In almost all jacks or better, deuces wild, and joker wild games, the

LONG-TERM %
If the payback of a machine is 101%, then, *over the long term*, you can expect to make a 1% profit on the money you risked. If the payback is 99%, then, *over the long term*, you can expect a 1% loss.

highest paying hand is a royal flush. The probability of making a royal flush is roughly one in 40,000. Therefore, in order to attain the long-term payback percentage, it is necessary to hit a royal flush an *average* of once in every 40,000 hands.

The catch in this statement is the word *average*. Although the average recurrence of a royal flush is every 40,000 hands, you might get your first royal after playing only 100 hands, or you may have to play 100,000 hands. That's the problem with long-term averages.

So what *is* the long term? For one, it depends on the game. In most non-progressive games, there is about a 95% statistical probability of hitting at least one royal flush in 120,000 hands. In progressive games, the jackpot hand is often a sequential royal flush. The probability of hitting a sequential is one chance in almost 5 million. Getting five aces of spades in Five Deck Frenzy is even more remote—one chance in 15 million.

SHORT-TERM PAYBACK

Only the professionals and the casinos should be concerned with long-term payback. To the rest of us, it doesn't have much meaning because all of our playing is over relatively short periods of time. Then why are all our payback numbers based on the long-term expectation? *Long term* means that the number of hands approaches infinity and has become the universal way of stating the payback.

Because we don't always know what short term means (is it 100 hands, 1000 hands, or 10,000 hands?), showing short-term paybacks on each individual payout schedule in the Payout Schedules chapter would be too cumbersome. Instead, this chapter gives corrections to the long-term paybacks of that chapter. Each table shows the downward correction that should be applied to the long-term payback percentage, depending on the number of hands played in a short-term session. You can still use the long-term payback numbers in the Payout Schedules chapter as a general comparison for deciding which games to play.

When you are figuring the number of hands in the following tables, you can combine all your short playing sessions to make a long one. This is statistically correct because the random number generator in a legal video poker machine does not have a memory. Each hand is from a random deal and is independent of previous events. This means that four one-hour sessions at four different machines is statistically the same as one four-hour session on one machine.

Let's say you are in Las Vegas for three days and you play video poker about 8 hours a day. If you average 400 hands an hour, which is a normal rate, then your three-day-long session would be:

400 hands per hour x 8 hours x 3 days = 9600 hands.

This is almost 10,000 hands. Thus, when you look at the tables to get an idea of your short-term payback, you can see that the reduction in long-term payback is about 1.5%, no matter which machine you play. If you played 25,000 hands, the correction would drop to about 0.7%.

The wide-area progressive schedules in the Payout Schedules chapter list two different payback percentages. One of them is the standard long-term payback. The other payback percentage disregards rare hands such as sequential royals and five aces of spades.

Except for Five Deck Frenzy, the difference between the two payback numbers is only about 0.3%. In Five Deck Frenzy, disregarding the five aces of spades reduces the payback by about one percent. To be realistic, you should only think about the lower payback, and if you get lucky and hit the progressive jackpot, consider it an unexpected windfall.

EXPLANATION OF THE TABLES

Each table has a column called "No. of Hands," which means the total number of hands played during your extended playing session. This extended playing session is as long as you care to define it and can cover any number of machines. You could define it as a day, a week, or a year. Most people will define it as the entire length of their holiday or vacation at a gambling resort. If your estimated number falls between two numbers on the table, just split the difference between the two percentages.

The BONUS QUADS table has two columns under "Percent Change," which show the 1-coin payouts for quad winners. Most bonus quads machines have three different payouts for quads, usually [Aces], [2s, 3s, or 4s], and [5s thru Kings]. If, on your machine, the 1-coin payouts for these three quads are neither 80/40/25 nor 160/80/50, then select the closest one.

The DEUCES WILD table has two columns under "Percent Change," which are the 1-coin payouts for quad deuces. If the 1-coin payouts for quad deuces on your machine are neither 200 nor 400, then select the closest one.

The JOKER WILD table has two columns under "Percent Change," which define the lowest hand in the payout schedule. In Joker Wild schedules, the lowest hand is almost always "Kings or Better" or "Two Pairs." Select the right one for your game.

HOW TO USE THE TABLES

This chapter contains tables of payback corrections for several categories of video poker games. The percentages in the tables are downward adjustments to the average long-term payback figures in the charts of the Payout Schedules chapter for combined playing sessions of 1000 to 50,000 hands.

To determine the length of a combined playing session, multiply the hours-of-play times the rate-of-play (400 hands per hour is an average rate of play). The hours of play can be cumulative over several days or weeks.

If the chart in the Payout Schedules chapter has more than one payback listed, always apply the short-term correction to the smallest payout amount (usually 4000 coins).

ORIGINAL JACKS OR BETTER	
No. of Hands	Percent Change
1000	-2.4
2500	-2.3
5000	-2.0
10000	-1.5
25000	-0.7
50000	0

BONUS QUADS
(JACKS OR BETTER)

Percent Change

No. of Hands	Quads = 80/40/25	Quads = 160/80/50
1000	-4.7	-7.0
2500	-3.0	-3.8
5000	-2.0	-2.0
10000	-1.5	-1.5
25000	-0.7	-0.7
50000	0	0

DEUCES WILD

Percent Change

No. of Hands	4 Deuces = 200	4 Deuces = 400
1000	-4.9	-8.1
2500	-3.7	-5.7
5000	-1.6	-1.6
10000	-1.4	-1.4
25000	-0.8	-0.8
50000	0	0

JOKER WILD

Percent Change

No. of Hands	Kings or Better	Two Pairs
1000	-5.7	-4.0
2500	-4.0	-2.5
5000	-3.2	-2.2
10000	-1.6	-1.4
25000	-0.7	-0.8
50000	0	0

STATISTICAL TABLES

The following tables give the odds of being dealt specific poker hands and the odds of drawing winning hands. Also given are the number of possible ways a particular poker hand can be made with a 52-card deck.

WAYS TO MAKE A HAND

The number of ways to make various poker hands is the basis for most statistical calculations in poker or video poker. Before the advent of computers, professional gamblers reckoned these numbers manually, or hired the services of a mathematician. If you don't know how it is done, the following examples may be enlightening:

Assuming a 52-card deck with no wild cards, let's see how many ways there are to make a straight flush. It is not too hard to visualize that, for a single suit, there are 10 ways. These are A-2-3-4-5, 2-3-4-5-6, 3-4-5-6-7, 4-5-6-7-8, 5-6-7-8-9, 6-7-8-9-10, 7-8-9-10-J, 8-9-10-J-Q, 9-10-J-Q-K, and 10-J-Q-K-A.

Multiply these 10 ways by 4 suits, and we arrive at a total of 40 ways. Four of these are royal flushes, so the number is usually given as 36 ways.

Another seemingly simple example would be four-of-a-kind (quad). Since there are four cards in every rank (one of each suit), and 13 ranks, there must be 13 unique quads. That is true, except we have to take into account the fifth card. If four cards out of the deck are used for the quad, there are 48 cards left, any one of which could be the fifth card. Therefore, to finish the calculation, we have to multiply the 13 quads by the 48 possibilities for the fifth card. Thus, 13 times 48 equals 624 ways.

This is pretty straightforward arithmetic, but when you get to the lower hands the calculations get more complicated and it is easier to overlook something. If you try to calculate the number of straights, for instance, don't forget to subtract the 40 straight flushes.

ODDS OF MAKING A HAND

So, why is the number of ways to make a hand important? For one, it is the basis for calculating the odds of being dealt a particular hand—and this is very important information for the professional poker player. Before we can do any further calculations, however, we need to know how many different 5-card hands can be dealt from a 52-card deck. This is calculated as follows:

$$\frac{52 \times 51 \times 50 \times 49 \times 48}{5 \times 4 \times 3 \times 2 \times 1} = 2{,}598{,}960 \text{ ways}$$

A mathematician would express this with a computational tool called *factorials*, but we will keep it as simple as possible. Now we can proceed with odds calculations.

To determine the odds of getting two pairs on the initial deal, for example, just divide 2,598,960 by 123,552 (from the first table). The result is approximately 21, which means there is one chance in 21 of getting two pairs. This is the method used to figure the odds for all the hands in the first table of this chapter.

EXPECTED VALUE

Expected value (EV) is a technique used by many gamblers to determine how to play a particular hand. If the EV is greater than one, the play has a positive expectation; if it is less than one, it has a negative expectation. Professional gamblers do not usually play a hand unless they believe it to have a positive expectation.

In video poker, EV is the average of all the possible outcomes of a particular draw, adjusted by the payouts for possible winning hands. These are not simple calculations. There are 32 ways to draw to a 5-card poker hand, so for every different hand, the EV has to be calculated 32 times in order to determine which is the best draw. Although many of these potential draws can be eliminated by observation, you can see that this is work for a computer.

EV is the basic technique used to mathematically determine the best strategy for playing a video poker hand. It is only mentioned here so that you understand what it is when you encounter the term in other books. It is also the technique used to devise the last three tables in this chapter.

THE TABLES

The following statistical tables show the frequency and probability of being dealt specific video poker hands. The first table is for an initial 5-card deal. It is based on a 52-card deck where the number of different possible 5-card hands is 2,598,960.

The next three tables show the odds of making specific hands on the draw for the games of Jacks or Better, Deuces Wild, and Joker Wild.

ODDS OF BEING DEALT A PARTICULAR HAND

The following table shows the number of possible ways to make certain hands and the odds of getting these hands in the first five cards that are dealt from a 52-card deck with no wild cards.

Hand	Possible Ways to Make Hand	Odds of Being Dealt Hand in First 5 Cards
Royal Flush	4	1 in 649,740
Straight Flush	36	1 in 72,193
Four Aces	48	1 in 54,145
Four of a Kind	624	1 in 4,165
Full House	3,744	1 in 694.2
Flush	5,108	1 in 508.8
Straight	10,200	1 in 254.8
Three of a Kind	54,912	1 in 47.3
Two Pairs	123,552	1 in 21.0
Pair of Aces	84,480	1 in 30.8
Jacks or Better	337,920	1 in 7.7
Any Pair	1,098,240	1 in 2.4
No Pair	1,302,540	1 in 2.0

ODDS OF MAKING A HAND ON THE DRAW

The following tables show the odds of making a particular hand on the draw for the indicated game categories. The odds shown are approximate. Exact odds depend on the specific game and the playing strategy used.

JACKS OR BETTER	
Hand	Odds of Making a Hand on the Draw
Royal Flush	1 in 40,200
Straight Flush	1 in 9,200
Four Aces	1 in 5,200
Four of a Kind	1 in 425
Full House	1 in 87
Flush	1 in 92
Straight	1 in 89
Three of a Kind	1 in 14
Two Pairs	1 in 8
Jacks or Better	1 in 5

DEUCES WILD

Hand	Odds of Making a Hand on the Draw
Natural Royal Flush	1 in 45,000
Four Deuces	1 in 4,800
Deuce Royal Flush	1 in 600
Five of a Kind	1 in 320
Straight Flush	1 in 250
Flush	1 in 55
Full House	1 in 45
Straight	1 in 17
Four of a Kind	1 in 16
Three of a Kind	1 in 4

JOKER WILD

Hand	Odds of Making a Hand on the Draw
Natural Royal Flush	1 in 42,000
Five of a Kind	1 in 10,800
Joker Royal Flush	1 in 9,600
Straight Flush	1 in 1,800
Four of a Kind	1 in 120
Full House	1 in 65
Flush	1 in 65
Straight	1 in 60
Three of a Kind	1 in 8
Two Pairs	1 in 9
Kings or Better	1 in 7

GLOSSARY

Ace – The highest-ranking card. May also be used as the lowest card in an A-2-3-4-5 straight or straight flush.

Ace high – A hand of mixed cards that contains one ace.

Ace kicker – A lone ace that is held (usually with a pair), when drawing replacement cards. Not a recommended strategy in video poker.

Aces up – Two pairs, with one of the pairs being aces.

Ante – In table poker, the chips put into the pot before the initial deal.

Betting interval – In table poker, the period during which each player has the right to bet, raise, or drop out.

Bluff – In table poker, a bet on a hand that the player does not think is the best.

CANCEL button – A button on a video poker machine that resets all the hold buttons and allows the player to make new hold/discard choices.

CASH OUT button – A button on a video poker machine that converts credits to coins.

Credits – Instead of paying out coins, video gambling machines keep track of winnings in the form of credits which can be converted to coins at any time by pressing the CASH OUT button. Instead of cashing out, accumulated credits can also be played by pressing either the BET ONE CREDIT or PLAY 5 CREDITS buttons.

DEAL button – A button on a video poker machine that directs it to deal the next hand.

DEAL-DRAW button – A button on a video poker machine that combines the functions of a deal button and a draw button.

Deuce – The two card.

Deuces wild – All four deuces in the deck are designated as wild cards. See *wild card*.

Discard – A card that is not held when drawing replacement cards.

DISCARD button – One of five buttons on a video poker machine that designates a card to be discarded when the draw occurs. These are the opposite of hold buttons and may appear on some older machines.

Draw – The action in draw poker during which cards are drawn from the deck to replace those that have been discarded by the players.

DRAW button – A button on a video poker machine that directs it to draw replacements for all the cards that were not held.

Draw poker — The game of closed poker in which there is a one-time opportunity to replace unwanted cards in the player's hand with new cards drawn from the deck.

Face card — A jack, queen, or king.

Five-of-a-kind — Five cards, all of the same rank. Since a standard deck has only four cards of each rank (one in each suit), this must include a designated wild card such as a deuce or a joker.

Flush — Five cards of the same suit.

Four-card royal — Four of the five cards needed for a royal flush.

Four-flush — Four of the five cards needed for a flush; four cards of the same suit.

Four-of-a-kind — Four cards of the same rank.

Four straight — Four of the five cards needed for a straight.

Full house — Three-of-a-kind and a pair.

Garbage hand — A hand of no potential value, that does not even contain a low pair.

Hand — The cards held by a player.

High card — A jack, queen, king, or ace.

High pair — A pair of jacks, queens, kings, or aces.

HOLD button – One of five buttons on a video poker machine that designates a card to be held (not discarded) when the draw occurs.

HOLD–CANCEL button – A button on a video poker machine that includes the function of a cancel button within each hold button.

House edge – The difference between the actual odds and the payoff odds, usually stated as a percentage, which is the mathematical edge the house has over the player.

House percentage – In a slot machine, the difference between the amount of money taken in and the amount paid out, over the long term. This difference is the casino profit.

Inside straight – Four of the five cards needed for a straight with a gap between the lowest and highest cards. The gap can be filled with a card of only one rank, or a total of four possible cards.

Jackpot – The largest payout on any particular machine.

Jacks or better – A game in which a pair of jacks is the lowest-paying hand.

Joker – An extra card in the deck that is designated as a wild card. See *wild card*.

Kicker – An unmatched card held in the hand when drawing replacement cards. Not a recommended strategy in video poker

Low pair – Any pair that does not pay. In jacks-or-better, low pairs are 2 through 10.

Megapoker – A statewide (Nevada) video poker game with a progressive jackpot that pays for a sequential royal flush.

Odds – The ratio of the number of ways to win versus the number of ways to lose.

Open-ended straight – Four cards in sequential rank which can become a straight if a card is added to either end. The straight can be completed with a card of either of two ranks, or a total of eight possible cards.

Outside straight – Same as an *open-ended straight*.

Pair – Two cards of the same rank.

Pat hand – A winning hand, as dealt, that does not require a draw.

Payback – The total long-term winnings as a percent of the total amount bet.

Payoff – The amount paid for a winning hand.

Payout – Same as *payoff*.

Pokermania – A citywide (Atlantic City) video poker game with a progressive jackpot that pays for a sequential royal flush in a specified suit.

Progressive jackpot – A group of machines are electrically connected to a common jackpot pool. As the machines are played, a small percentage of the money paid in by the players is diverted to the jackpot pool, which continues to grow until someone wins it. The jackpot is then reset to its minimum value and the growth cycle repeats itself.

Quads – Another term for four-of-a-kind.

Random number generator – A program algorithm within a video poker machine's microprocessor that continually generates pseudo-random numbers. The main program accesses these numbers to assure that the cards are always dealt randomly.

Rank – The ordinal position of each card within a suit, determining its value. The lowest rank is the deuce and the highest is the ace. In a straight or a straight flush, an ace may also be used as the lowest card.

Royal flush – A ten, jack, queen, king, and ace, all of the same suit.

Sequential royal flush – A royal flush in which the five cards are displayed on the video screen in rank sequence as: 10-J-Q-K-A or A-K-Q-J-10, depending on how the particular machine defines it.

Showdown – The point in a table poker game when the hands of all active players are exposed and compared to determine who wins the pot.

Single-ended straight – Four of the five cards needed for a straight in a sequence that is open at only one end. Specifically: A-2-3-4 or J-Q-K-A. The straight can be completed with a card of only one rank, or a total of four possible cards. Also called *inside straight*.

STAND button — A button on a video poker machine that automatically puts a hold on all five cards.

Straight — Five cards of consecutive rank, with mixed suits.

Straight flush — Five cards of consecutive rank, all of the same suit.

Suit — The name of one of the four families of 13 cards that make up a standard deck. The four suits are: spades, hearts, clubs, and diamonds.

Three-of-a-kind — Three cards of the same rank.

Triplets — Another term for three-of-a-kind. Also called *trips*.

Two pairs — Two cards of the same rank and two cards of another rank.

Wide-area progressive — A progressive jackpot machine that is part of a city-wide or state-wide network that interconnects with hundeds of other machines.

Wild card — A card, such as a joker, that may be designated as any other card to improve the hand, even if that card already appears in the hand. For instance, a hand containing four kings and a wild card would be considered five-of-a-kind.

Wrapped royal — A sequential royal flush that can begin with any card and can be in either direction, such as Q-K-A-10-J. Also called Wrap-a-Royal.

POWERFUL WINNING POKER SIMULATIONS
A MUST FOR SERIOUS PLAYERS WITH A COMPUTER!
IBM compatible CD ROM Win 95, 98, 2000, NT, ME, XP

These incredible full color poker simulations are the best method to improve your game. Computer opponents play like real players. All games let you set the limits and rake and have fully programmable players, stat tracking, and Hand Analyzer for starting hands. MIke Caro, the world's foremost poker theoretician says, "Amazing... a steal for under $500... get it, it's great." Includes free phone support. "Smart Advisor" gives expert advice for every play!

1. TURBO TEXAS HOLD'EM FOR WINDOWS - $59.95. Choose which players, and how many (2-10) you want to play, create loose/tight games, and control check-raising, bluffing, position, sensitivity to pot odds, and more! Also, instant replay, pop-up odds, Professional Advisor keeps track of play statistics. Free bonus: Hold'em Hand Analyzer analyzes all 169 pocket hands in detail and their win rates under any conditions you set. Caro says this "hold'em software is the most powerful ever created." Great product!

2. TURBO SEVEN-CARD STUD FOR WINDOWS - $59.95. Create any conditions of play; choose number of players (2-8), bet amounts, fixed or spread limit, bring-in method, tight/loose conditions, position, reaction to board, number of dead cards, and stack deck to create special conditions. Features instant replay. Terrific stat reporting includes analysis of starting cards, 3-D bar charts, and graphs. Play interactively and run high speed simulation to test strategies. Hand Analyzer analyzes starting hands in detail. Wow!

3. TURBO OMAHA HIGH-LOW SPLIT FOR WINDOWS - $59.95. Specify any playing conditions; betting limits, number of raises, blind structures, button position, aggressiveness/passiveness of opponents, number of players (2-10), types of hands dealt, blinds, position, board reaction, and specify flop, turn, and river cards! Choose opponents and use provided point count or create your own. Statistical reporting, instant replay, pop-up odds high speed simulation to test strategies, amazing Hand Analyzer, and much more!

4. TURBO OMAHA HIGH FOR WINDOWS - $59.95. Same features as above, but tailored for Omaha High only. Caro says program is "an electrifying research tool...it can clearly be worth thousands of dollars to any serious player." A must for Omaha High players.

5. TURBO 7 STUD 8 OR BETTER - $59.95. Brand new with all the features you expect from the Wilson Turbo products: the latest artificial intelligence, instant advice and exact odds, play versus 2-7 opponents, enhanced data charts that can be exported or printed, the ability to fold out of turn and immediately go to the next hand, ability to peek at opponents hand, optional warning mode that warns you if a play disagrees with the advisor, and automatic mode that runs up to 50 tests unattended. Tough computer players vary their styles for a great game.

---

6. TOURNAMENT TEXAS HOLD'EM - $39.95

Set-up for tournament practice and play, this realistic simulation pits you against celebrity look-alikes. Tons of options let you control tournament size with 10 to 300 entrants, select limits, ante, rake, blind structures, freezeouts, number of rebuys and competition level of opponents. Pop-up status report shows how you're doing vs. the competition. Save tournaments in progress to play again later. Additional feature allows quick folds on finished hands.